Marriage Is Not the Option to Get a Green Card Anymore

By Ruth Michel Dupoux

Legal Disclaimer

The author is not an attorney. This book is provided for educational and informational purposes only and does not constitute legal advice. Immigration laws and policies change frequently, and outcomes depend on individual facts and circumstances.

Readers are responsible for verifying all information with official sources such as USCIS.gov or consulting a licensed immigration attorney. The author and publisher assume no responsibility for actions taken based on the information in this book.

"With God all things are possible."

— Matthew 19:26

"For I know the plans I have for you," declares the Lord, "plans to prosper you and not to harm you, plans to give you hope and a future."
— Jeremiah 29:11

An Empowerment Guide for Every Immigrant Seeking Truth, Faith, and Freedom.

Marriage Is Not the **Option to Get a Green Card Anymore**

Motto

The Legacy of Purpose

You came here not by chance, but by purpose. America opened its doors to you, walking through them with humility and strength. Do not be a burden; be a blessing. Do not break the law; build within it. Become an asset to your community, a helper to the needy, a leader to others, and an example for those who will follow. Work hard, live in gratitude, and let your success be your testimony of faith. Always believe in God, for He is the one who brought you here and He will never abandon you on your journey.

Lady R, Ruth Michel Dupoux

Marriage Is Not the **Option to Get a Green Card Anymore**

Ruth Michel Dupoux

LRC & CO GROUP

USA IMMIGRATION SECRETS

LRC IMMIGRANT ACADEMY

ISBN : 979-8-3482-7330-9

All reasonable efforts have been made to ensure the accuracy of the information contained within this publication. However, the author and publisher assume no responsibility for any errors or omissions.

The material presented in this book is for **educational and informational purposes only**. It is based on publicly available information from official U.S. government sources, including USCIS (U.S. Citizenship and Immigration Services), DHS (Department of Homeland Security), and related government agencies. Readers are encouraged to verify all legal references directly from official sources.

Marriage Is Not the **Option to Get a Green Card Anymore**

Dedication to My Mother

After God, this book belongs to my mother the woman whose strength, courage, and love shaped me into the person I am today. You are the source of my resilience and the reason I never gave up. You taught me that nothing in this world can stop me from achieving my dreams. Your faith, your sacrifices, and your unwavering belief in me have been my foundation. I dedicate this book to you, Mom, with all my heart.

Marriage Is Not the **Option to Get a Green Card Anymore**

Contents

Acknowledgments.....13

Who This Book Is For.....15

About the Author.....17

Preface.....19

Definition of Marriage.....23

Introduction.....25

The Myth of the Marriage Green Card Dream.....27

Stories of Suffering.....31

The Cost of Fake Marriages.....37

Abuse, Blackmail, and Broken Souls.....43

There Is a Better Way: The EB Employment-Based Green Cards.....49

How to Apply for the EB-1 Self-Petition Green Card.....59

The EB-1 Self-Petition Green Card Becoming Extraordinary on Paper.....65

How to Apply for the EB-2 National Interest Waiver.....73

Employment-Based Green Cards That Require Sponsorship.....79

Professions That Can Qualify for the EB-1 Self-Petition.....89

The Right Careers That Commonly Qualify for EB-2 NIW Self-petition.....99

Important Legal Clarification for Overstays and Unlawful Entry.....109

The Waiver of Inadmissibility: A Second Chance Through Form I-601 or I-601A 115

How to Become an Asset in the System to Qualify for the EB Category Self-Petition Green Card 121

My Personal Commitment to Become an Asset....129

Faith, Truth, and Patience....131

Conclusion: Choose Freedom, Not Fear....133

Introduction to the Immigrant's Prayers 135

The Immigrant's Morning Prayer (For Strength and Divine Protection)...137

The Immigrant's Night Prayer 139

The Immigrant's Prayer for Strength While Waiting 141

The Immigrant's Prayer for Victory and New Beginnings 143

From the Author's Heart 145

The End....147

Disclaimer and Source Information 149

Acknowledgments

First and foremost, I thank God for His mercy, wisdom, and divine timing. Every word in this book is guided by faith, and every lesson is a reminder that grace can turn pain into purpose.

To my beloved mother, whose strength and courage built the foundation of who I am today, this book is dedicated to you first. You are the woman who taught me faith, resilience, and self-belief. You made me understand that nothing in this world can stop me from achieving my dreams, and for that, I will honor you for the rest of my life.

To my father, thank you for your love and guidance. To the rest of my family, your constant support has carried me through every challenge and victory.

To every immigrant who shared their story with me, your courage became the heartbeat of this book. You reminded me that no journey is too hard when it is walked in truth.

To my community and all those who fight daily for justice, fairness, and dignity, thank you for being my inspiration. You are proof that hope lives wherever determination stands.

May this book serve as a light, a tool, and a companion to everyone striving for a better life while honoring God, law, and legacy.

— Ruth Michel Dupoux (Lady R)

Marriage Is Not the **Option to Get a Green Card Anymore**

Who This Book Is For

This book is for every soul who has ever felt trapped, silenced, or unseen while fighting for a place to belong. It is for the immigrant who came to America with nothing but faith, courage, and a dream and refuses to let fear shape their destiny.

This book is for women living in toxic marriages, whose voices have been pushed down, whose strength has been ignored, and whose dreams have been placed on hold because someone else held "the papers." This is for the woman who prays quietly at night, asking God for a way out without losing herself.

This book is for victims of manipulation, for those who have survived emotional abuse, financial control, blackmail, or fear-based relationships disguised as "help." It is for the ones who were promised love but received power, control, and silence instead.

This book is for people who feel stuck without options those who believe that their only path to a green card is through someone else's signature, approval, or mood. It is for the ones who think they must choose between dignity and survival.

This book is for students, dreamers, entrepreneurs, professionals, nurses, caretakers, artists, and innovators who want to build their own future with integrity. For those who are ready to rise through their talent, their skill, and their purpose, not through fear.

This book is for the immigrant who wants to do things the right way, the honest way, the independent way. For the one who wants freedom, not dependency. For the one who carries purpose in their hands and destiny in their heart.

And most of all, this book is for you the reader whose life is about to change.

You are not alone. You are not powerless. You are not invisible.

Your story is just beginning, and your future is already blessed.

About the Author

Ruth Michel Dupoux is an entrepreneur, author, immigrant advocate, and inspirational leader whose journey embodies resilience and reinvention. Born in Haiti and raised with the values of hard work, faith, and service, Ruth came to the United States with a vision: to help others find lawful, dignified paths to success.

She is the founder of **LRC & CO Group** and the **LRC Immigrant Academy**, where she mentors and empowers immigrants to navigate complex systems, build businesses, and become assets to their communities.

As a mentor and coach, Ruth guides women in building businesses, mastering leadership skills, and finding strength in faith and purpose. She helps women reclaim their financial freedom, discover their voice, and build a life that honors their worth and potential. Through her work, Ruth uplifts women, encouraging them to become independent, confident, and self-sufficient. She believes no woman should ever feel trapped, controlled, or defined by a man. Instead, she teaches women to build their own foundations, claim their freedom, and walk with dignity. Her voice also reaches men, guiding them toward integrity, respect, and purpose. Ruth believes that every woman carries the blueprint of her own success, she just needs the courage to build it.

Her first book, *USA Immigration Secrets*, became a guiding light for immigrants seeking to understand and succeed within the U.S. immigration system. This second book, *Marriage Is Not the Option to Get a Green Card Anymore*, continues her mission to expose myths, bring truth to light, and offer hope through lawful, independent solutions.

Ruth's life is her altar, a testimony of faith, persistence, and gratitude. Every achievement, every lesson, and every word she shares is dedicated to God, her mother, and the countless immigrants who believe that doing things the right way is the only way.

Preface

This book was born from truth, sometimes painful, sometimes liberating, but always necessary.

For years, I listened to stories of men and women who came to the United States with dreams of freedom, only to find themselves trapped by fear, misinformation, or dependency. Many believed marriage was the only path to stability, that love, or sometimes survival, had to be exchanged for papers. I wrote this book to break that illusion.

I did not write this book from theory. I wrote it from experience, from the nights of fear, the mornings of uncertainty, and the long days when I wondered if my name would ever stand on solid ground in a country that promises opportunity yet demands endurance.

Like many immigrants, I once believed that love, luck, or marriage were the only doors to freedom. I heard it whispered in communities, repeated in waiting rooms, and passed down like an unspoken law: *"If you marry, your problems will disappear."* But I learned, painfully, personally, and professionally that this path often leads to disappointment, control, or heartbreak.

I have seen women and men tie their futures to someone else's paperwork, only to lose themselves in the process. I've seen genuine love manipulated by fear, and marriages destroyed by the pressure of immigration stress. I've met countless individuals strong, intelligent, and capable who believed they had no power outside of someone else's signature.

And yet, I've also seen the opposite: the strength that rises when truth enters the room. I've watched immigrants reclaim their voice, rebuild their lives, and walk into legal freedom with faith and dignity, not because they were married, but because they were determined, informed, and persistent.

That is why I wrote this book.

Marriage Is Not the Option to Get a Green Card Anymore is more than information, it's a revelation. It's the truth that many were afraid to speak: **you do not need to give your body, your peace, or your destiny to earn your place in this country.** Your intelligence, your skills, your purpose, they are enough. There are lawful paths. There are options. There are ways to rise that don't require compromise.

I have walked through the system myself, filing forms, studying immigration law, helping others build petitions, and watching miracles unfold through knowledge and faith. As a paralegal, I've seen how preparation and precision can change lives. But as a woman of faith, I've seen how prayer and divine favor can move mountains that paperwork alone cannot.

This book is not meant to shame anyone who chose marriage. It's meant to *free* those who feel trapped by that idea. It's for the woman who cries quietly at night because she thought her only worth was in being "sponsored." It's for the man who gave everything to a relationship that promised stability but delivered control. It's for every immigrant who has ever said, "I just want to do it the right way."

Through each chapter, you will find truth, resources, and encouragement, not written by a stranger, but by someone who has stood where you stand. You will learn how the immigration system works, the meaning of self-petition, and how to build your own foundation through categories like **EB-1**, **EB-2 NIW**, and humanitarian waivers without fear, without shame, and without dependency.

I wrote this book because I believe in you, in your courage, your talent, and your divine assignment. You came to this land not by accident, but by design. And no matter how hard your path has been, there is a way forward that honors your dignity and your destiny.

If you are holding this book, it means you are ready, ready to walk in truth, ready to learn, and ready to claim the freedom that already belongs to you. My hope is that every word in these pages gives you clarity, strength, and peace.

This is more than immigration guidance, it's a movement of liberation. Because the real green card is not just a document; it's the freedom to live without fear, the courage to stand in your own power, and the faith to believe that your future is still in God's hands.

With love, truth, and unwavering faith,

Ruth Michel-Dupoux Entrepreneur,

Paralegal, Author, and Immigrant Advocate

Marriage Is Not the **Option to Get a Green Card Anymore**

Definition of Marriage

Before we dive into the pain, disappointment, and trauma that can occur when marriage becomes a tool for immigration, it's important to first understand what marriage truly is and what it was meant to be. Marriage, in its purest form, is a sacred union between two people built on love, trust, mutual respect, and partnership. It is not a contract of convenience or a transaction for personal gain it is a lifelong commitment to build, support, and grow together.

A genuine marriage is meant to be a place of safety, not fear. It's where two individuals unite their dreams and resources, share responsibilities, and face challenges as a team. Love, compassion, honesty, and respect are the foundation. Each partner supports the other emotionally, financially, and spiritually. It is about building a family, creating stability, and nurturing a shared vision for the future.

When marriage is entered for the wrong reasons out of pressure, desperation, or financial exchange it loses its essence. It becomes a deal, not a devotion. True marriage is about partnership, not power. It thrives on equality and selflessness, not control or manipulation. When this sacred bond is abused or used as a shortcut to legal status, both the meaning of love and the integrity of the immigration process are violated.

Understanding the true definition of marriage is the foundation for this entire discussion. Only when we understand what marriage *should be* can we fully recognize how devastating it becomes when it is twisted into something transactional or coercive.

Introduction

For decades, marriage has been seen by many immigrants as the most direct and accessible route to obtaining permanent residency in the United States. Across generations and continents, this belief has passed from one person to another whispered in homes, shared in fear, and often seen as the only way to belong. But behind this illusion lies a painful truth.

Countless men and women have paid a heavy price emotionally, psychologically, spiritually, and even legally by tying their hopes of legal status to someone else's decisions, moods, or threats. Many came to this country filled with dreams, only to find themselves trapped in relationships built on control rather than love, on fear rather than faith.

Some were promised a future, only to be abandoned after years of waiting for paperwork that never came. Others lived under constant emotional blackmail being told, *"If you leave me, I'll cancel your papers,"* or *"You'll be deported without me."* In their quest for freedom, they found a new kind of prison.

This book is for the woman who prays every night for courage to walk away, for the man who feels powerless under manipulation, for the immigrant who wonders if freedom must always come at such a painful cost.

Here, we will confront the truth about the "marriage for papers" dream not to condemn, but to heal. We will talk about the consequences of fraud, the emotional scars of dependency, and most importantly, the legal and spiritual paths that lead to real freedom.

Because there **is** another way. A way that honors your dignity, your talent, and your purpose. A way that does not depend on anyone's signature but your own courage to act.

This book will open your eyes to the employment-based green card categories **EB-1, EB-2, EB-3, and the EB-2 NIW** opportunities designed for people who contribute, create, and inspire. You will learn how education, skill, and service can become your bridge to permanent residency.

But beyond the paperwork and policies, this book is about something deeper **redemption**. It's about finding your voice after silence, your strength after suffering, and your faith after fear.

This is not a story of judgment; it is a story of rebirth. It is proof that you can lose everything and still rebuild stronger, wiser, and free.

So take a deep breath, open your heart, and remember you are not alone. No matter how hard your journey has been, your story is not over. A new chapter of faith, truth, and freedom is waiting for you.

Let's begin where most stories begin **with a dream.**

Chapter 1

The Myth of the Marriage Green Card Dream

For generations, the idea that *"if you marry a U.S. citizen, everything will be fine"* has been planted in the hearts of countless immigrants. It's a phrase whispered by friends, relatives, and even strangers who mean well but don't understand the cost of such advice.

In many communities, this belief grew out of survival. People saw someone's cousin, neighbor, or friend who "got their papers fast" after getting married, and they began to believe that love or at least the appearance of it was the safest path to security. The rumor spread like wildfire across borders and oceans, carried by hope and fear in equal measure.

But behind this illusion, there is a silent truth. Thousands of men and women have discovered that the so-called green-card marriage dream can turn into a nightmare of emotional imprisonment, dependency, and quiet suffering.

The Illusion of Safety

At first, it feels comforting to think that love can save you. You imagine a wedding, a future, a promise of peace. But reality is often more complicated.

For some, marriage became a **bargain of power, a relationship** where one person holds all the control because the other fears deportation. Every argument becomes a threat. Every delay in paperwork turns into emotional blackmail. The immigrant partner begins to live in constant anxiety, measuring every word and action, terrified to lose both love and status at once.

Some sleep beside someone who calls them *"illegal."* Some work endless hours to support a partner who reminds them daily, *"You need me to stay here."* And many cry silently in their rooms, praying for the strength to endure one more day.

The Emotional Chains

A marriage built on fear instead of love creates invisible chains. The immigrant learns to apologize even when they've done nothing wrong. They beg for signatures instead of affection. Their life becomes paperwork instead of partnership.

Each day brings new humiliation and an insult brushed off because "you don't want problems," a threat that keeps you from leaving. The heart starts to break, piece by piece, until you no longer recognize the person in the mirror.

And the saddest part? Most endure this pain in silence. They tell no one, because they fear judgment or deportation. They live between two prisons, one of love and one of law.

Cultural Pressure and Desperation

In many cultures, marriage is not only a romantic act, it's proof of worth, stability, and success. Families back home say, *"Just marry someone there; it's easier."* Communities pressure single immigrants to find "a way out."

But when marriage becomes a **means of survival** rather than a bond of love, it loses its beauty and sacredness. It becomes a transaction, a silent trade between fear and control.

This emotional and cultural pressure drives people into marriages that were never meant to happen, unions built on fear instead of faith.

When Dreams Turn to Nightmares

The American dream is supposed to symbolize freedom. But for many immigrants trapped in toxic marriages, it becomes a daily reminder of pain. The dream of belonging turns into the fear of being discarded.

Some lose years of their lives waiting for a spouse to file paperwork that never comes. Others are forced to choose between **abuse and deportation**. Still others pay a heavy price losing their faith, their peace, and their dignity.

This is not just about broken relationships; it's about **broken spirits**. The very system that was meant to protect love has become, for many, a weapon of power and control.

Reclaiming Freedom

But freedom is possible. The first step is understanding that the **American dream should never cost your self-worth**. Love should be a partnership not a visa strategy. True success begins the moment you realize you don't need anyone to define your future.

You have the right to live with dignity, to love without fear, and to build your life on truth, not illusion.

God did not bring you to this land to beg for love or permission. He brought you here to rise, to contribute, and to walk on purpose. The real green card is not found in another person's approval, it's found in your courage to stand on your own.

Chapter 2

Stories of Suffering

When Love Becomes a Cage

Every immigrant comes to America with a dream: the dream of freedom, dignity, and opportunity. But for too many, that dream is stolen in silence, replaced with fear and emotional captivity inside marriages that were supposed to bring hope.

Behind the closed doors of homes across America, countless immigrants both women and men are living invisible lives of suffering. Their smiles hide their pain. Their silence hides their fear. And every night, they pray for a miracle for a way out without losing everything they've fought for.

Maria's Story: The Price of Hope

Maria came from the Dominican Republic, full of ambition and faith. She met an American man who promised to love her and "help her fix her papers." At first, she felt blessed that God had finally answered her prayers.

But months after the wedding, the man she thought loved her became someone else. He took her phone, her keys, and even her freedom to speak to family. Every time she disagreed with him, he reminded her,

> "Without me, you're nothing here."

When she cried, he laughed. When she begged for her green card, he said she needed to "earn it." Maria spent three years in that house washing, cooking, smiling through bruises all for a promise that never came.

The day she finally left, she had nothing but her passport and her faith. But for the first time, she also had peace.

This story highlights the importance of independence and informed decision-making in immigration matters.

Jean's Story: The Silent Man

Jean came from Haiti. He was kind, hardworking, and full of hope. He met a U.S. citizen who seemed to understand his struggles. But after marriage, everything changed.

She mocked his accent, his clothes, and his culture. When he wanted to send money to his family, she said, "You're my husband, not theirs." And when he talked about adjusting his status, she used it as a weapon:

> "Don't forget who's in charge here."

Jean stayed because he was afraid. He thought leaving meant losing everything. But over time, he realized he had already lost himself. One day, he walked into a church, and a pastor said something that changed his life:

> "God cannot bless a lie."

That night, Jean packed his things and left. It was the first honest act of faith he had made in years.

This story highlights the importance of independence and informed decision-making in immigration matters.

Sofia's Story: The Manipulated Promise

Sofia was a college graduate from Mexico. She came to the U.S. on a student visa, full of dreams to start her career. When she fell in love with a U.S. citizen, she thought it was destiny.

But soon, her husband began to use her immigration status as control. He refused to file her paperwork unless she obeyed him. He told her that if she ever left, she would be "deported back to poverty."

For years, Sofia endured humiliation until she found out about **VAWA**. It was her lifeline. She filed a self-petition quietly, without her husband's knowledge, and with the help of community advocates, she finally became a permanent resident on her own terms.

When she received her approval letter, she wept. Not because she finally had her papers, but because she had her dignity back.

This story highlights the importance of independence and informed decision-making in immigration matters.

The Invisible Pain

For every Maria, Jean, or Sofia, there are thousands of others living this pain right now. People who cook dinner with tears in their eyes, who smile for photos but hide bruises under their sleeves. People who stay not out of love, but out of fear of being homeless, deported, or forgotten.

They are not weak. They are survivors. They are immigrants who believed in love and were betrayed by manipulation.

Some endure emotional abuse, others financial or sexual control. And the saddest part is that many feel they can't speak up because their entire future is tied to the one who hurts them.

A Cycle That Must Be Broken

This book exists because silence is no longer an option. Too many lives have been lost to despair, depression, and even suicide because people believed that marriage was their only way to belong.

We must talk about it. We must tell the truth not to shame, but to save. Because the truth is that **your immigration status should never determine your worth**.

Freedom begins the moment you realize that your papers don't define you, your courage does. You can rebuild. You can rise. You can find love again this time, real love that doesn't hurt or hold power over you.

Faith Beyond the Pain

If you are reading this and you see yourself in these stories, take this as your sign: **you are not alone**. God sees every tear you've cried in secret. He knows every fear you've hidden, every insult you've endured, and every time you've prayed for strength.

Your story is not over. The pain you carry now can become the purpose that sets you free. You can start again and this time, you can do it in truth, in faith, and with dignity.

Because God doesn't bless fear. He blesses courage. And today, you are choosing courage.

Marriage Is Not the **Option to Get a Green Card Anymore**

Chapter 3

The Cost of Fake Marriages

When Desperation Becomes a Dangerous Gamble

Some people come to America with nothing but hope and hope can be both a blessing and a weakness. When doors seem closed, and fear whispers that time is running out, even good people can make desperate choices. One of the most dangerous is entering a **fake marriage** for a green card.

At first, it seems like a shortcut. Someone says, *"I can help you. Just pay me, and we'll pretend we're married."* The plan looks simple: sign a few papers, take some pictures, act like a couple, and one day you'll have your green card. But what starts as a deal quickly becomes a nightmare.

The Hidden Reality

Fake marriages are not harmless. They are **federal immigration fraud, a serious** crime under U.S. law. If USCIS (U.S. Citizenship and Immigration Services) finds out, both people can face **up to five**

years in prison, a $250,000 fine, and a permanent ban from future immigration benefits.

But beyond the law, there is a deeper kind of punishment: the emotional, mental, and spiritual cost of living a lie.

Every time you lie to the government, to your family, or to yourself, something inside of you dies a little. You lose your peace. You wake up every morning afraid of being caught. You check your mail with trembling hands. You live in constant fear, not freedom.

When Money Buys a Lie

There are often predators who make a business out of immigrants' desperation. They promise, "Pay me, and I'll marry you." They know you're scared. They know you just want to belong. But after taking your money, they vanish or, worse, blackmail you.

They threaten to report you if you don't pay more. They demand more money or even sexual favors. And because you know you broke the law, you feel you can't tell anyone.

What started as a shortcut to freedom becomes a road to fear. You no longer trust anyone. You live in guilt and shame, always looking over your shoulder.

The Legal Consequences

U.S. immigration officers are trained to detect fraud. They know when a relationship is fake. They ask detailed questions about the color of your toothbrush, your spouse's job, your in-laws' names, your living habits. They check photos, social media, and addresses.

If they find inconsistencies, they may open an investigation, deny your petition, or even deport you. And once you are flagged for fraud, it never disappears. It follows your record for life.

Even if you later marry for love, USCIS can deny you, saying you once entered a fraudulent marriage. This may affect future immigration options depending on the case..

The Emotional Cost

Fraud doesn't just break the law, it breaks the spirit. You begin to feel unworthy. You stop believing in yourself. You no longer feel proud when you look in the mirror because you know deep down that your dream is built on deceit.

The guilt becomes heavy. It separates you from your faith, your family, and your purpose. You can't even pray with peace because you know you're asking God to bless a lie.

Many people who went through fake marriages end up depressed, lonely, or even suicidal. The emotional damage can last long after the papers are denied.

The Spiritual Lesson

God cannot bless what is built on deceit. You may fool people, but you can never fool your own soul. The same God who opens doors will never require you to sin to enter.

When you choose honesty, you might wait longer but what you gain is real. It lasts. It brings peace. When you choose fraud, you might move faster but what you build will crumble.

This chapter is not here to condemn anyone who has made mistakes. It's here to remind you that **forgiveness and redemption are possible**. If you've ever been tempted or have already fallen into that trap, you can still start over. You can choose to do things the right way.

The Way Back

If you once entered a fake marriage or were part of an immigration fraud, you can take steps to rebuild your path:

- **Repent and be honest with yourself and God.** Acknowledge the mistake, ask for mercy, and start again with integrity.
- **Do not repeat it.** Learn from it and promise yourself that your next decision will be guided by truth.
- **Seek redemption through service.** Use your story to warn others. Turn your experience into wisdom.
- **Explore lawful options.** You may still qualify for other categories like the EB-2 NIW, asylum, or humanitarian protection, depending on your situation.

The moment you choose truth, you reclaim your power. You are no longer a prisoner of fear, you are a builder of your own destiny.

A Message of Mercy

We all make mistakes. Some out of ignorance, some out of desperation, and some out of fear. But remember this:

> God is not a God of punishment He is a God of restoration.

He doesn't count how many times you fell; He counts how many times you got back up. Your immigration story may have started with pain, but it can end with purpose.

Do not be ashamed of your past. Learn from it, rise from it, and help others avoid the same road. Because the real green card you're looking for is not just in your passport it's in your peace, your purpose, and your faith.

Marriage Is Not the **Option to Get a Green Card Anymore**

Chapter 4

Abuse, Blackmail, and Broken Souls

When Love Becomes a Weapon

Not every scar is visible. Some people walk through life smiling, laughing, working and yet their souls are covered in bruises that no one can see. For many immigrants who believed that marriage would bring stability, the cruel truth is that they traded one form of fear for another.

Behind closed doors, too many live in silence afraid to speak, afraid to leave, afraid to lose everything. The pain of depending on a spouse for legal status creates a dangerous imbalance of power. The one with citizenship controls not just the home, but the other person's entire existence.

The Silent Prison

When your right to stay in a country depends on someone else's mood, every day feels like walking on thin ice. You start to measure your words carefully. You smile even when you want to scream. You say "thank you" when you're insulted, and you apologize for things you never did because you're terrified of hearing,

> *"I'll call immigration if you don't behave."*

These words break a person's spirit. The victim begins to live two lives: one for the outside world, and one in silence behind the walls where love has turned to control.

Abusers know this power. They use it. They remind their spouse, "You're nothing without me." They hold the green card like a weapon. They delay filing papers just to keep control. And every day, the victim loses more of their confidence, their joy, their voice.

The Many Faces of Abuse

Abuse doesn't always mean bruises. It can be **psychological**, when someone isolates you, mocks your accent, or destroys your self-esteem. It can be **financial**, when they take your money, hide documents, or forbid you from working. It can be **sexual**, when they force intimacy or use your vulnerability to humiliate you. It can be **verbal**, when they call you "illegal," "worthless," or remind you constantly that you don't belong.

Each form leaves a wound, and together they build a prison without bars.

Many immigrants endure this for years, thinking it's better than deportation. But what they don't realize is that **they already have rights**. There are legal paths that protect victims of abuse and exploitation without needing the abuser's help or consent.

The Violence Against Women Act (VAWA)

A Law That Restores Dignity

In 1994, the U.S. government passed the **Violence Against Women Act (VAWA)** a law designed to protect victims of abuse, regardless of gender. Despite its name, **VAWA is not only for women.** It protects **any immigrant man or woman who has been abused by a U.S. citizen or green card holder.**

Under VAWA, you can file your own petition (Form I-360) in secret without your abuser's knowledge or approval. You can apply for your green card independently.

To qualify, you must show that:

- You are or were married to a U.S. citizen or permanent resident.
- You lived with the abuser at some point.
- You suffered physical, emotional, or psychological abuse.
- You are a person of good moral character.

Once approved, you can apply for **work authorization**, **public protection**, and eventually **permanent residency.**

VAWA is not just paperwork, it is justice. It tells the abused immigrant, *"You are not powerless. You have a voice. You are protected by law."*

The U Visa: Hope for Victims of Crime

Not every story of abuse happens within a marriage. Many immigrants suffer violence, exploitation, or sexual assault from others employers, neighbors, or strangers and are afraid to report it because they fear deportation.

The **U Visa** was created for victims of certain serious crimes who have suffered physical or mental harm and are willing to help law enforcement.

You may qualify for a U Visa if:

- You were a victim of a qualifying crime (domestic violence, sexual assault, kidnapping, human trafficking, etc.).
- You suffered substantial physical or emotional harm.
- You have information that can help police or prosecutors.
- You are helpful or willing to be helpful in the investigation or prosecution.

A U Visa gives you **legal protection**, **work authorization**, and the chance to apply for a **green card after three years.** It transforms victims into survivors and restores their faith in justice.

Stories of Strength

Nathalie's Story: Nathalie from Haiti married a man who promised to help her "get papers." Instead, he used her fear to control her. He would lock her in the house and say, *"If you call the police, you'll be deported."* When she finally found the courage to report the abuse, a church advocate told her about VAWA. Nathalie filed her petition quietly. Two years later, she received her green card. She now works as a caregiver, helping other women find courage to leave abusive homes.

Luis's Story: Luis, from El Salvador, was beaten by his employer after reporting unpaid wages. Too scared to go to the police, he stayed silent until a community center told him about the U Visa. He cooperated with investigators, applied, and today he has legal status and peace of mind.

These stories show that no matter how deep the pain, there is always a way forward through courage, truth, and faith.

Healing After Abuse

Surviving abuse is not just about leaving, it's about **healing**. Healing means learning to trust again, to breathe again, to look in the mirror and see strength instead of shame.

It may take time, but it's possible. You can find therapy through immigrant support centers, churches, and nonprofit organizations that specialize in trauma recovery. And every small step speaking up, asking for help, choosing to live in truth is an act of power.

Remember:

> You did not come this far to be broken. You came here to rebuild, to rise, to become a testimony of faith and freedom.

If you are in immediate danger, contact local authorities or a trusted support organization.

Faith and Rebirth

God sees every tear you've cried. He knows every insult, every bruise, every threat. He never wanted you to live in fear. He wanted you to live on purpose.

So if you are reading this, know this truth: You are not a victim, you are a survivor. You are not undocumented you are destined. You are not forgotten, you are chosen.

VAWA and the U Visa are not just laws; they are instruments of mercy. They are proof that God can use even the justice system to heal His children.

Your freedom begins when you believe again not in people, but in yourself and in God

Chapter 5

There Is a Better Way: The EB Employment-Based Green Cards

For many years, thousands of immigrants have believed that marrying a U.S. citizen is the easiest or fastest way to get a green card. But in truth, America provides many legal paths that reward ***skills, education, community service, and contribution***, not relationships. These are the ***Employment-Based (EB) green card categories*** powerful tools that recognize your ***independence, resilience, and purpose.***

The EB categories prove one important fact:

> You don't need to marry to stay, you can build, serve, and earn your place with dignity.

Let's explore how.

Understanding the EB Categories

The United States created a system to invite and retain the world's best talents, thinkers, innovators, and workers. These visas are divided into ***five main employment-based categories (EB-1 through EB-5)***. This chapter focuses on the first three, the most accessible for self-made immigrants.

Each of these categories gives immigrants the opportunity to apply based on ***who they are and what they can offer the country***, not who they married.

EB-1: The Extraordinary Ability Category

The ***EB-1A*** visa is designed for individuals who have reached the top of their field. It's for dreamers who became doers for artists, leaders, scientists, professors, athletes, business innovators, and performers who have gained national or international recognition.

To qualify, you must show that you've made a ***significant impact*** in your field and can continue to contribute to the U.S. at a high level.

Examples of qualifying evidence include:

- Awards or honors for excellence.
- Press features or public recognition.
- Membership in professional associations that require outstanding achievement.
- Publications, media appearances, or exhibitions.
- Letters of recommendation from leaders in your industry.

Unlike most visas, the EB-1A allows you to ***self-petition*** meaning you don't need an employer or sponsor. You are your own advocate.

Who can qualify?

- An actor or filmmaker with global exposure.
- A researcher whose studies have influenced public policy.
- A professional athlete who has competed internationally.
- An entrepreneur who has built a successful company that creates jobs in the U.S.

God gives each person a gift. The EB-1A rewards those who have used that gift to make a difference in their industry and beyond.

EB-2: The Path for Professionals and Experts

The ***EB-2*** category recognizes people with ***advanced degrees or exceptional ability*** in their profession. You may qualify if you hold a ***master's or higher degree***, or if you can prove ***expert-level skill*** through your experience, even without formal education.

This category values those who have invested in learning and developing teachers, doctors, engineers, administrators, architects, and more.

Typical examples include:

- A civil engineer helping improve U.S. infrastructure.
- A healthcare worker or nurse addressing shortages in medical care.
- A university professor mentoring the next generation of leaders.

- A skilled consultant supporting small business growth.

For many, the EB-2 is the foundation for another special category the ***EB-2 National Interest Waiver (NIW).***

EB-2 NIW: The National Interest Waiver Freedom to Self-Petition

This is one of the most empowering immigration options for self-reliant people. The ***EB-2 NIW*** allows you to apply without needing a job offer or employer. Instead, you show that your work benefits the United States ***as a whole*** economically, culturally, scientifically, or socially.

The U.S. government waives the normal "job offer" requirement because your work is so meaningful that it serves the national interest.

To qualify, you must prove three key points:

1. ***Substantial Merit and National Importance:*** Your work matters not just for you or your employer, but for the greater good.
2. ***You're Well-Positioned to Advance It:*** You have the skills, experience, and plan to continue your work successfully.
3. ***It Benefits the Nation to Waive the Job Offer:*** The U.S. gains more by letting you keep doing your work freely than by forcing traditional employment sponsorship.

Examples of strong NIW candidates include:

- A public health nurse improving access to care in underserved areas.

- An immigrant entrepreneur helping local communities with job creation.
- An environmental expert developing clean energy solutions.
- A social worker helping immigrant families transition and integrate.

EB-3: Skilled Workers, Professionals, and Essential Labor

The ***EB-3*** category honors people who may not have advanced degrees but contribute essential skills to the economy. From skilled trade workers to caregivers, these individuals are the backbone of American industry.

You may qualify if you:

- Have at least two years of job experience or training (Skilled Worker).
- Hold a bachelor's degree or equivalent (Professional).
- Perform essential but unskilled labor (Other Worker).

Although this category requires employer sponsorship, it's a reminder that every honest job whether in construction, hospitality, or caregiving adds value to this country.

Stories of Real People and Hope

Maria's Story (EB-2 NIW): *Maria, a nurse from Haiti, worked tirelessly in community health centers. When she discovered the NIW option, she applied using evidence of her volunteer work, letters from supervisors, and data on how her care improved patient outcomes. Her petition was approved she became a permanent resident on her own terms.*

Luis's Story (EB-1A): *Luis, an architect from the Dominican Republic, had designed award-winning green buildings. He compiled his awards, media articles, and a letter from his country's Minister of Urban Development. USCIS approved his EB-1A, recognizing his global contribution to sustainable design.*

Nadia's Story (EB-3): *Nadia came to the U.S. as a caregiver for seniors. Her employer sponsored her EB-3 petition after seeing her commitment. She now runs her own assisted-living business and employs others.*

Jonas's Story (EB-2): *Jonas, an engineer from Africa, used his degree and ten years of experience to qualify for EB-2. Today, he leads infrastructure projects that improve water access in rural American towns.*

Each story shares the same message: ***faith, honesty, and perseverance always win.***

Preparing Your EB Petition Step by Step

Know Your Strengths. Identify your career, achievements, and contributions.

1. ***Gather Evidence.*** Collect diplomas, awards, press features, licenses, or proof of projects.
2. ***Request Letters of Recommendation.*** Choose respected professionals who can verify your impact.
3. ***Write a Personal Statement.*** Explain your journey, mission, and how your work benefits the U.S.
4. ***Stay Organized.*** Present your petition clearly and every document should support your story.
5. ***Keep the Faith.*** The process takes time, but patience and integrity bring peace and lasting success.

A Message of Hope: Build, Don't Beg

You were not brought to this country to live in fear or dependence. You were brought here to build, contribute, and rise.

The employment-based categories exist because America recognizes those who bring ***value, integrity, and innovation***. You don't have to marry to stay. You don't have to sacrifice your dignity. You can succeed legally, respectfully, and confidently by believing in your purpose and walking by faith.

> "Don't be a burden; be a builder. Don't wait for someone to save you and become the one who changes your story."

God opens doors, but you must walk through them with courage.

Comparison of the EB Categories

Category	Main Requirement	Sponsorship Needed	Best For
EB-1A	Extraordinary ability	No	Artists, actors, scientists, innovators
EB-1B	Outstanding professors/ researchers	Yes	Academic leaders
EB-1C	Multinational executives/ managers	Yes	Corporate leaders

EB-2	Advanced degree/ exceptional ability	Yes	Educated professionals
EB-2 NIW	National interest contribution	No	Independent changemakers
EB-3	Skilled or professional work	Yes	Essential workers

Stories of Hope and Success

- **Ana**, a nurse from the Caribbean, applied under EB-2 NIW after organizing free health clinics for immigrant families. Her work demonstrated "national importance" and she earned her green card independently.
- **Carlos**, an engineer from Latin America, developed eco-friendly materials for construction. He filed his own NIW petition, showing how his innovation aligned with U.S. infrastructure goals.
- **Aisha**, a community leader and teacher, created language programs for immigrant children. Her EB-2 NIW petition highlighted her direct contribution to education and inclusion.

Each of them found dignity through independence. None needed to depend on a spouse; they became their own sponsors through faith, skill, and perseverance.

Marriage Is Not the **Option to Get a Green Card Anymore**

Chapter 6

How to Apply for the EB-1 Self-Petition Green Card

A. What Is the EB-1 Green Card?

The EB-1 category also called the *"Green Card for Aliens of Extraordinary Ability"* is designed for individuals who have reached the very top of their field. It recognizes those whose talent and impact go beyond borders. Unlike other employment-based visas, **the EB-1 allows you to self-petition** you don't need an employer, a sponsor, or a marriage to apply. Your achievements speak for you.

This path is ideal for professionals, artists, entrepreneurs, scientists, athletes, and community leaders whose work has national or international significance.

B. The Three EB-1 Subcategories

The EB-1 category is divided into three main groups:

1. **EB-1A – Extraordinary Ability:** For individuals who can demonstrate extraordinary ability in sciences, arts, education, business, or athletics through sustained national or international acclaim. No job offer or labor certification required.

2. **EB-1B – Outstanding Professors and Researchers:** For professors or researchers with international recognition in their field and at least three years of experience. Requires an employer or institution to sponsor.

3. **EB-1C – Multinational Executives or Managers:** For executives or managers who have worked for a multinational company abroad and are being transferred to the U.S.

This chapter focuses on **EB-1A**, because it's the **only subcategory that allows self-petition.**

C. Who Qualifies for EB-1A

To qualify for EB-1A, you must show **extraordinary ability** proven by **one major achievement** (such as an international award or Olympic medal) **or** by meeting **at least three of ten USCIS criteria**, such as:

- Receipt of lesser nationally or internationally recognized awards.
- Membership in associations that demand outstanding achievement.
- Published material about you or your work in major media.

- Participation as a judge or expert in your field.
- Original contributions of major significance.
- Authorship of scholarly articles.
- Display of your work in exhibitions or showcases.
- Leading or critical role in distinguished organizations.
- High salary compared to peers.
- Commercial success in performing arts or creative industries.

USCIS also considers the **totality of your evidence** how all your achievements together prove that you're at the top of your field.

D. The Step-by-Step Process

1. **Gather Your Evidence** Start by collecting every proof of your accomplishments: press articles, certificates, awards, photos of events, recommendation letters, contracts, and leadership documentation.

2. **Prepare Your Petition Letter (Form I-140)** This is the foundation of your case. It should tell your story, describe your field, your impact, your recognition, and explain how your work benefits the United States. You'll submit this letter along with **Form I-140**, the *Immigrant Petition for Alien Worker.*

3. **Include Strong Reference Letters** You'll need 5–7 letters from experts, professors, or professionals who can verify your impact and reputation. These should highlight your originality, influence, and leadership in your domain.

4. **Organize Your Exhibits** Divide your evidence into labeled sections (Exhibit A, B, C, etc.) corresponding to each eligibility criterion, making it easy for USCIS officers to review.

5. **Submit to USCIS** Mail your full EB-1A package (I-140 form, petition letter, evidence, and fee) to the appropriate USCIS service center. You can file **with Premium Processing** to get a decision within 15 days.

6. **File Adjustment of Status (Form I-485)** If you're already in the U.S. and your priority date is current, you can file **Form I-485** (Green Card application) simultaneously with the I-140, or after it's approved. Include **Form I-765** for a work permit and **Form I-131** for advance parole (travel authorization).

E. Cost and Processing Time

- **Form I-140 fee:** $715
- **Premium Processing (optional):** $2,805
- **Form I-485 fee:** $1,440 (includes biometrics)
- **Average timeline:** 3–12 months (faster with Premium Processing)

F. Building Your Extraordinary Profile

If you're not ready yet, start building your profile today. Publish your work, collaborate internationally, join associations, speak at events, and document your influence. Build a **digital presence** your website, media coverage, or portfolio helps prove your visibility and credibility.

Extraordinary ability isn't about fame it's about **proof of impact**.

G. Why It Matters

The EB-1A is the highest-level self-petition visa reserved for those who rise beyond their limitations, who create change, and who inspire others through their work. It's the ultimate symbol of independence **you become your own sponsor**.

For every immigrant who has been told, *"You can't do it without marriage or a job offer,"* the EB-1A is proof that excellence is enough. You are enough.

Marriage Is Not the **Option to Get a Green Card Anymore**

Chapter 7

The EB-1 Self-Petition Green Card Becoming Extraordinary on Paper

A. The Power of the EB-1A Category

The EB-1A, officially called the **"Employment-Based First Preference Alien of Extraordinary Ability,"** is the highest self-petition category in the U.S. immigration system. It was created to allow **individuals at the top of their field** to immigrate to the United States **based solely on merit**, without needing an employer or a U.S. citizen spouse.

If you can **prove that you are among the Among a small percentage recognized at the top of their field** in your field through documented evidence of achievements, awards, recognition, or media coverage you can petition **for yourself**, sign your own petition, and obtain permanent residency.

B. What "Extraordinary Ability" Really Means

"Extraordinary ability" doesn't mean you must be world-famous. It means that your **talent, career, or contribution has made a significant impact** nationally or internationally and that this can be verified by independent sources.

USCIS defines it as **"a level of expertise indicating that the individual is one of that small percentage who has risen to the very top of the field of endeavor."**

So, if you've:

- **Created something original** that others use, quote, or imitate,
- **Won awards** or been featured in respected publications,
- **Led organizations, projects, or events** in your field,
- **Been invited to judge or evaluate others' work**,
- **Earned high income or recognition compared to peers**, then you may qualify.

C. Real-World Examples of EB-1A Self-Petitioners

- **Dr. Lina Zhang**, a biomedical researcher from China, obtained her Green Card after publishing 12 scientific papers cited by others worldwide. She included citations, letters from professors, and photos of her presenting at conferences.

- **Carlos Ramirez**, a Latin American filmmaker, showed that his documentaries had won film festival awards and were screened internationally. He added articles written about his films and letters from critics and organizers.
- **Marie Joseph**, a Haitian entrepreneur and fashion designer, proved her extraordinary ability through awards received at Caribbean fashion shows, articles in *Le Nouvelliste* and *Caribbean Fashion Week Magazine*, and partnerships that promoted Haitian design globally.
- **Kwame Osei**, an African tech innovator, presented patents, interviews with tech magazines, and evidence that his mobile app was downloaded in 40 countries.

Each of them **self-petitioned**, without a sponsor or company and were approved.

D. The Legal Foundation

Your EB-1A self-petition is based on **Section 203(b)(1)(A) of the Immigration and Nationality Act (INA)**. You file **Form I-140**, Petition for Alien Worker, under this category.

You do not need:

- A job offer
- Labor certification (PERM)
- Employer sponsorship

You **do** need to prove that you will **continue to work in your field of extraordinary ability** once you become a resident for example, by including business plans, letters of intent, or contracts.

E. The Ten USCIS Criteria

To qualify, you must either:

- Provide **one major internationally recognized award** (like an Oscar, Pulitzer, Nobel Prize), **or**
- Meet **at least three** of the following **ten criteria:**

#	Criterion	Real Example
1	**Lesser nationally or internationally recognized prizes or awards**	Fashion designer winning "Caribbean Designer of the Year" or "Miami Cultural Impact Award."
2	**Membership in associations requiring outstanding achievement**	Member of "American Academy of Design" or "International Entrepreneur Network" where admission is selective.
3	**Published material about you or your work**	Articles in *The Miami Herald*, *Caribbean Today*, *Forbes Africa*, or interviews on TV and radio.
4	**Judging the work of others**	Invited as a judge for competitions, panels, fashion shows, or academic evaluations.
5	**Original contributions of major significance**	Created a brand, innovation, or method that influenced your industry e.g., a patented product, viral campaign, or published research.

6	**Authorship of scholarly articles**	Wrote and published articles or books cited by others, even online or academic platforms like Google Scholar.
7	**Display of your work at artistic exhibitions or showcases**	Exhibiting paintings, products, or designs in galleries, trade fairs, or public shows.
8	**Leading or critical role in a distinguished organization**	CEO, creative director, or team leader at a recognized company, NGO, or government project.
9	**High salary or remuneration compared to peers**	Contracts, pay stubs, or earnings showing above-average income in your field.
10	**Commercial success in performing arts or creative fields**	Streaming revenue, ticket sales, chart rankings, or social media reach.

You need solid, third-party evidence for at least **three** of these, but strong applicants often show five or more.

F. The EB-1A Petition Package Step by Step

1. Prepare the Petition Letter

This is your personal statement and legal argument in one. It must:

- Introduce who you are and your field of expertise.
- Explain how you meet each criterion (with exhibits).
- Highlight your impact and future benefit to the U.S.
- Reference laws, cases, and USCIS memos.

Most successful EB-1A letters are **15–25 pages**, structured by criteria, and written in a professional tone like a legal brief.

2. Organize Your Evidence

Create a clear exhibit list (Exhibit A, B, C...). Each exhibit should correspond to one claim. Example:

- Exhibit A – Copy of Award Certificate
- Exhibit B – Newspaper Article
- Exhibit C – Invitation Letter as Guest Judge
- Exhibit D – Photos of Event
- Exhibit E – Testimonials and Recommendation Letters

3. Obtain Strong Recommendation Letters

Letters should come from **recognized experts** not just friends or colleagues. They must describe:

- Your achievements,
- How your work has influenced others,
- Why are you among the top professionals in your field?

Aim for **5–7 letters**, including at least two from outside the U.S.

4. File Form I-140

Submit your **petition to USCIS** along with:

- Form I-140

- Filing fee (...)
- Petition letter + exhibits
- Passport copy and résumé
- Proof of intent to continue work in your field

Optional: Add **Form I-907 (Premium Processing)** for the fee asking to get a decision in **15 calendar days.**

5. File Adjustment of Status (if in the U.S.)

If your EB-1A is current (check the **Visa Bulletin**), you may **file Form I-485** for your Green Card at the same time or after approval. Include **Form I-765** (work permit) and **Form I-131** (advance parole).

G. Common Mistakes to Avoid

1. **Submitting weak evidence** (like social media screenshots without credible sources).
2. **Letters from non-experts** or personal friends.
3. **No clear organization** USCIS officers must find everything easily.
4. **Not showing future work plans** always include a statement of intent or project.
5. **Using generic templates** USCIS prefers personalized, specific evidence and wording.

H. Processing Time & Fees (2025 Estimates)

Form	Purpose	Fee	Time
I-140	Petition for Alien Worker	$1315	3–12 months
Premium Processing (I-907)	Optional 15-day response	$2,805	15 days
I-485	Adjustment of Status	$1,440	8–16 months
I-765	Work Authorization	$260	2–4 months
I-131	Advance Parole	$630	2–4 months

I. Why the EB-1A Self-Petition Is a Game-Changer

This category embodies **freedom**. You are not tied to a marriage, not waiting on an employer, not dependent on luck. Your **talent becomes your pathway to residency**.

It's the ultimate answer to the myth that immigrants must "marry or be sponsored" to stay. Your achievements, your story, your excellence those are your keys.

As the USCIS puts it, the EB-1A is for those "who have risen to the very top of their field." So, build your case, organize your evidence, and prove it because you can.

Chapter 8

How to Apply for the EB-2 National Interest Waiver

Once you realize you don't have to depend on anyone else to build your future, the next step is learning how to move forward the right way. Freedom is not just about leaving something behind it's about stepping into purpose with clarity and courage. The pain of your past can become the blueprint for your success if you choose to build on it instead of being buried by it.

The **EB-2 NIW** is more than paperwork; it is a declaration of independence. It's the bridge between your dreams and your destiny, a petition that says, *"My work matters, and I am ready to serve this nation."* Through this path, you are not asking for pity or permission; you are presenting proof of your worth, your contribution, and your potential.

For every immigrant who once believed their only option was marriage or sponsorship, the EB category offers a new vision, one rooted in skill, service, and self-determination. It is the modern immigrant's way of saying, *"I belong here because I am building here."*

Step 1 Understand the Purpose of the NIW

The NIW exists to invite people whose contributions benefit the **national interest** of the United States. It's not about perfection it's about **purpose.** If your work improves lives, strengthens communities, advances science, or adds cultural or economic value, you already have a foundation to qualify.

Ask yourself:

- *Who benefits from what I do?*
- *Have I created or contributed to something that helps others?*
- *If I left tomorrow, what would the U.S. lose?*

Your honest answers form the soul of your petition.

Step 2 Gather Evidence of Your Impact

Every petition must be supported by credible, organized evidence. Think of your file as a **book about your life's work.**

Collect documents that show:

- **Education and Credentials**: Diplomas, certificates, licenses.
- **Professional Experience**: Employment letters, contracts, portfolios, or project records.
- **Accomplishments**: Awards, press coverage, testimonials, or proof of innovation.
- **Community Impact**: Volunteer work, outreach, or programs that improved others' lives.

- **Publications or Media Mentions**: Articles written by or about you.

Each piece of evidence tells USCIS, *"This person is already making a difference."*

Step 3 Write Your Personal Statement

Your personal statement (or "petition letter") is your voice on paper. It should read like a testimony clear, confident, and heartfelt.

Include:

- **Your Journey:** Where you came from and what inspired your work.
- **Your Mission:** What drives you to keep serving or innovating.
- **Your Impact:** The measurable ways your work helps communities or the U.S. economy.
- **Your Future Vision:** How you plan to continue contributing once your petition is approved.

Speak truthfully. The government isn't just approving a form it's believing in your story.

Step 4 Secure Strong Recommendation Letters

Letters of recommendation are powerful. They confirm that your influence is real.

Seek letters from:

- Supervisors, professors, or mentors familiar with your work.
- Community leaders or professionals who have witnessed your impact.
- Partners or clients who benefited from your service or innovation.

Each letter should:

- Describe your achievements in detail.
- Explain how your work serves U.S. interests.
- End with confidence that your continued presence benefits the country.

Step 5 Prepare and File Form I-140

Form I-140 is the official petition that requests classification under the EB-2 NIW category. When filing, include:

1. The completed and signed **Form I-140**.
2. Filing fee (check current fee on USCIS.gov).
3. Your **personal statement**.
4. All **supporting evidence** (academic, professional, impact documents).
5. **Recommendation letters**.

Once USCIS receives your petition, you'll get a **Receipt Notice** confirming your case is under review.

Step 6 Understand Next Steps After Approval

If your I-140 is approved, congratulations that's a major victory! But remember, **approval of the petition does not automatically grant lawful status.** To get your green card, you must either:

- File **Form I-485 (Adjustment of Status)** if you're in the U.S. and legally eligible, **or**
- Complete **Consular Processing** if you're outside the country or not eligible to adjust.

If you have overstayed or entered without inspection, you may need a **waiver (Form I-601 or I-601A)** before you can adjust. This is where patience and preparation matter but with faith and diligence, you will reach your destination.

Step 7 Stay Faithful and Focused

Many give up halfway because the process feels long. But remember *every file delayed is not denied.* Sometimes God uses waiting seasons to strengthen you, teach you patience, and refine your vision.

Keep updating your work, improving your skills, and collecting proof of your impact while your petition is pending.

Words of Encouragement

The EB-2 NIW is more than a visa. It's a symbol of **freedom through faith and integrity**. It's proof that you can succeed without compromising your values or depending on someone else's mercy.

You are not here by mistake. You were chosen to be part of this land's story not as a follower, but as a **builder**.

> *Walk boldly in truth, believe in your value, and let your work speak louder than your fears. The door is open to claim your future.*

Chapter 9

Employment-Based Green Cards That Require Sponsorship

A. Understanding Sponsored Green Cards

Not everyone qualifies for a self-petition like the EB-1A or EB-2 National Interest Waiver. Most professionals in the United States obtain permanent residency through **employer sponsorship** when a company, university, or institution officially supports their immigration process.

These categories recognize **skilled workers, professionals, professors, executives, and investors** who fill critical roles in the U.S. economy. The process is longer and more bureaucratic than a self-petition, but it remains a solid and legitimate path to a Green Card especially for people with stable employment or job offers.

B. The Five Employment-Based Categories

The U.S. immigration system divides employment-based immigration into **five preference categories (EB-1 through EB-5).** Only the EB-1A and EB-2 NIW allow self-petition. The rest **EB-1B, EB-1C, EB-2 PERM, EB-3, EB-4, and EB-5** generally require a sponsor, a company, or an institutional petitioner.

Let's go through each one clearly.

C. EB-1B: Outstanding Professors and Researchers

For whom: University professors or researchers internationally recognized in their field, with **at least three years of teaching or research experience.**

Who sponsors: A **U.S. university or research institution** must file the petition on your behalf.

Requirements:

- Permanent job offer from the U.S. institution.
- Evidence of international recognition (publications, citations, conference presentations).
- Proof of experience and contribution to academic development.

Example: Dr. Jean-Paul Etienne, a Haitian scientist, was offered a tenure-track position at a U.S. university. His institution sponsored him under EB-1B by presenting his research publications, citation index, and awards from the Caribbean Science Congress.

D. EB-1C: Multinational Managers or Executives

For whom: Corporate leaders who have worked **at least one year abroad** for a multinational company and are transferred to a **U.S. branch, subsidiary, or affiliate** in a managerial or executive role.

Who sponsors: The **U.S. branch of the company** petitions for the employee.

Requirements:

- One full year of employment with the foreign company within the last three years.
- Continuing employment in a managerial or executive position in the U.S.
- Proof of the corporate relationship between the foreign and U.S. entities.

Example: Nadia Toussaint was a senior marketing manager at a telecommunications firm in Haiti. When the company opened a Florida branch, they transferred her to manage U.S. operations. The company filed an **EB-1C** petition showing corporate registration documents, payroll records, and her executive role.

E. EB-2 (PERM) Professionals with Advanced Degrees or Exceptional Ability

For whom: Individuals with **a master's degree or higher**, or a **bachelor's plus five years of progressive experience**, in a specialty occupation.

Who sponsors: A **U.S. employer** who can prove there are **no qualified U.S. workers available** for that job.

Steps involved:

1. **PERM Labor Certification (Form ETA-9089):** The employer must first advertise the job publicly and prove to the Department of Labor that no U.S. workers were willing, qualified, or available.

2. **Form I-140 (Immigrant Petition):** Filed by the employer after PERM approval.

3. **Form I-485 (Adjustment of Status):** Filed by the employee when the visa becomes available in the Visa Bulletin.

Example: Marie-Claude Pierre, an architect, was hired by a Miami construction firm. The firm posted her job nationally, got no qualified applicants, obtained PERM certification, and then filed her **EB-2** petition with proof of her master's degree and portfolio of projects.

F. EB-3: Skilled Workers, Professionals, and Other Workers

For whom:

- **Skilled Workers:** At least 2 years of training or experience.
- **Professionals:** Bachelor's degree or equivalent.
- **Other Workers:** Less than 2 years of experience in unskilled labor.

Who sponsors: A **U.S. employer** offering a full-time, permanent position.

Process:

- Employer obtains **PERM Labor Certification** from the Department of Labor.
- Then files **Form I-140**.
- Once approved and the visa is current, the applicant files **Form I-485**.

Example: Jean-Louis François, a Haitian mechanic, was offered a position at an auto company in Georgia. The company proved there was a shortage of trained mechanics, obtained a PERM approval, and sponsored him for an **EB-3 Skilled Worker** visa.

G. EB-4: Special Immigrants

For whom: This category covers several special groups that are not based on typical job offers but still require institutional or organizational sponsorship.

It includes:

- Religious workers (priests, pastors, missionaries)
- Broadcasters working for international media
- Certain employees of U.S. government abroad
- Juveniles under court protection (SIJ)
- Certain members of the U.S. armed forces

Who sponsors: Usually a **religious organization** or **U.S. government agency.**

Example: Pastor Claudel Saint-Hilaire was invited by a U.S. church to serve as a full-time minister. The church filed an **EB-4 Religious Worker** petition, proving his ordination, experience, and religious duties.

H. EB-5: Immigrant Investor Program

For whom: Foreign investors who make a significant financial investment in a **new U.S. business** that creates jobs for at least **10 full-time U.S. workers.**

Investment threshold (2025):

- **$1,050,000** in a regular area, or
- **$800,000** in a targeted employment area (rural or high-unemployment zone).

Who sponsors: Technically self-sponsored, but the applicant must **invest through a U.S. business or regional center.**

Example: Ruth D. Michel, an entrepreneur, invested $850,000 into a healthy food manufacturing business in Florida employing 14 workers. Her accountant and attorney prepared an **EB-5** petition showing proof of investment, job creation, and lawful fund sources.

I. Key Differences Between Self-Petition and Sponsored Categories

Category	Self-Petition?	Requires Job Offer?	Requires PERM?	Example of Beneficiary
EB-1A	☑ Yes	✖ No	✖ No	Independent artist, entrepreneur, or researcher
EB-1B	✖ No	☑ Yes	✖ No	University professor
EB-1C	✖ No	☑ Yes	✖ No	Multinational executive

EB-2 NIW	☑ Yes	✖ No	✖ No	Public health or community-impact entrepreneur
EB-2 PERM	✖ No	☑ Yes	☑ Yes	Architect, engineer, or IT specialist
EB-3	✖ No	☑ Yes	☑ Yes	Mechanic, nurse, or skilled worker
EB-4	✖ No	☑ Yes	✖ No	Pastor or missionary
EB-5	❁ Investment-based	✖ No	✖ No	Investor or entrepreneur

J. How Employers Sponsor Foreign Workers

1. **Job Offer & Contract:** The employer must commit to offering a permanent, full-time position.
2. **Prevailing Wage Determination:** The Department of Labor sets a wage that must be paid to the foreign worker.
3. **Recruitment Process (for PERM):** The employer must advertise and show that no U.S. workers are available.
4. **File PERM and I-140:** Once PERM is certified, the employer files the I-140 petition.
5. **Visa Bulletin Wait:** The worker must wait until the visa becomes current based on their country and category.

6. **Adjustment of Status (I-485):** Once the visa number is available, the employee applies for the Green Card.

K. Reality Check The Sponsored Route

The sponsored categories are legitimate but **depend on someone else's support.** If you lose your job or your employer withdraws the petition, the process stops. That's why self-petition categories like **EB-1A** and **EB-2 NIW** empower immigrants to **stand independently.**

Still, many people succeed through sponsorship especially nurses, engineers, professors, or religious workers because their employers value their contribution.

The key is understanding **which category truly fits your situation** and planning strategically. Immigration is not luck it's strategy, evidence, and persistence.

Marriage Is Not the **Option to Get a Green Card Anymore**

Chapter 10

Professions That Can Qualify for the EB-1 Self-Petition

The **EB-1A (Employment-Based First Preference – Alien of Extraordinary Ability)** is a U.S. immigration category that allows individuals with **exceptional achievements and national or international recognition** to apply for a **green card without needing a job offer, employer, or sponsor.**

The EB-1A is often called the **Extraordinary Ability Self-Petition**, because it honors people who have reached the **top of their field** in areas such as **science, education, business, athletics, or the arts.** These individuals demonstrate that their talent and contributions have a lasting impact and that their continued work will benefit the United States.

To qualify, an applicant must prove **"sustained national or international acclaim."** This can be done by showing **one major award** (like a Nobel Prize or Oscar) or by meeting **at least three of ten USCIS criteria**, which measure evidence such as awards, publications, leadership, media coverage, judging others' work, high earnings, or other recognized achievements.

In simple terms, the EB-1A is designed for professionals who have not only succeeded personally but whose **influence, creativity, or leadership has shaped their field** in a meaningful way, whether through innovation, public recognition, or international contribution.

A. Not Just for Scientists and Celebrities

Many people think the EB-1A is only for Nobel Prize winners, Olympic athletes, or Hollywood stars. That's false. The truth is, **extraordinary ability can exist in any field** science, art, business, sports, or education as long as you can *prove* measurable excellence and influence beyond your local environment.

The U.S. government does not define "field of endeavor" narrowly. That means a **fashion designer**, a **community leader**, a **chef**, or a **digital entrepreneur** can all qualify if their work creates national or international impact.

B. The Five Major Fields USCIS Recognizes

USCIS considers the following broad areas for EB-1A eligibility:

7. **Sciences** – research, medicine, technology, engineering.
8. **Arts** – performing arts, visual arts, music, film, literature, fashion.
9. **Education** – professors, trainers, academic leaders.
10. **Business** – entrepreneurs, executives, innovators, consultants.
11. **Athletics** – professional and competitive sports.

Within each of these areas, thousands of unique careers may qualify. Let's explore examples.

C. Science and Technology Professions

Ideal for: Researchers, medical experts, inventors, data scientists, or engineers whose work is cited, patented, or implemented globally.

Examples of profiles that succeed:

- A biomedical researcher with published studies in international journals.
- An engineer who developed sustainable construction methods used by multiple countries.
- A software developer who built an app downloaded worldwide.
- A public health specialist whose campaigns were adopted by foreign governments.

Evidence typically used:

- Peer-reviewed publications and citation index reports.
- Awards from scientific organizations.
- Recommendation letters from professors or research directors.
- Media coverage about the invention or discovery.

Case illustration: Dr. Grace Mendez, originally from the Dominican Republic, created a low-cost medical diagnostic tool adopted in three countries. She self-petitioned with documentation of her patents, WHO recognition letters, and scientific media articles and was approved under EB-1A.

D. Arts, Culture, and Media

Ideal for: Artists, musicians, actors, designers, photographers, writers, and film producers with recognized influence in their industry.

Examples of eligible careers:

- Fashion designers featured in international fashion weeks.
- Musicians with albums available on major platforms or international tours.
- Filmmakers whose work was screened or awarded at festivals.
- Writers or poets published in multiple countries.
- Choreographers or stage directors with national recognition.
- Visual artists exhibited in galleries or museums.

Evidence typically used:

- Press coverage and interviews.
- Awards, festival selections, and exhibition catalogs.
- Invitations to perform, judge, or speak at events.
- Sales records, streaming reports, or gallery contracts.

Case illustration: Marie Joseph, a Haitian fashion designer, was featured in *Caribbean Fashion Week* and *Vogue Italia's online spotlight for Caribbean designers.* Her collections were worn by international artists. She submitted press articles, photos, awards, and endorsement letters from fashion critics and won EB-1A approval.

E. Education and Academia

Ideal for: Professors, academic researchers, educational reformers, or curriculum innovators.

Examples of suitable roles:

- University professors with published research.
- Education consultants known for innovative teaching models.
- Authors of textbooks or training materials used nationally.
- Leaders in academic associations or international conferences.

Evidence typically used:

- Peer-reviewed articles and conference presentations.
- Leadership roles in educational organizations.
- Awards for teaching or curriculum design.
- Testimonials from academic institutions.

Case illustration: Dr. Samuel Eugene, an educator from Cameroon, created a literacy program implemented in 12 African schools and recognized by UNESCO. His EB-1A petition included letters from education ministries and media reports about his program's results.

F. Business and Entrepreneurship

Ideal for: Founders, innovators, executives, consultants, or professionals whose work has shaped markets, created jobs, or influenced industries.

Examples of qualifying profiles:

- Entrepreneurs whose companies operate internationally.
- Business consultants featured in professional magazines or media.
- Marketing or branding experts whose campaigns reached millions.
- Financial analysts, real-estate developers, or innovators with measurable results.
- Tech startup founders with patents or investor recognition.

Evidence typically used:

- Business registration and revenue proof.
- Awards or recognitions for business excellence.
- Press releases, interviews, and client impact statements.
- Speaking engagements or invitations as judges or experts.

Case illustration: Carlos Pineda, a Peruvian digital marketing strategist, was recognized for helping Latin American startups reach the U.S. market. His EB-1A petition included Forbes Latino interviews, keynote invitations, and case studies showing measurable economic growth. He was approved in under three months with premium processing.

G. Sports and Athletics

Ideal for: Athletes, trainers, coaches, or sports professionals with international participation or recognition.

Examples:

- Professional soccer or basketball players.
- Olympic or national team athletes.
- Coaches of winning teams or athletes.
- Fitness experts with international competitions or certifications.
- Martial arts champions or founders of a recognized training program.

Evidence typically used:

- Medals, championships, or national ranking records.
- Media articles and interviews.
- Team contracts and letters from sports federations.
- Proof of judging or training other elite athletes.

Case illustration: Andre Louis, a Haitian martial arts champion, proved extraordinary ability through five international gold medals and global training workshops. His petition included photos, awards, and letters from federations resulting in EB-1A approval.

H. Emerging and Unconventional Fields

In recent years, USCIS has accepted EB-1A petitions from **modern, digital, and creative industries** such as:

- Social media influencers and digital content creators.
- YouTubers, podcasters, or digital educators with millions of followers.

- Environmental activists or community reformers whose initiatives gained national press.
- Culinary artists or chefs featured on TV or in international publications.
- Wellness and holistic experts recognized by professional institutions.

Example: Chef Nancy Desir, known for introducing probiotic Haitian cuisine, documented her international workshops, TV appearances, and awards for innovation in gastronomy. She used those materials to support her EB-1A self-petition as a "culinary innovator."

I. What All Successful EB-1A Careers Have in Common

Regardless of the field, every approved EB-1A petition demonstrates three shared elements:

1. **Recognition:** Media, awards, or public acknowledgment of excellence.
2. **Impact:** Concrete evidence that your work changed, inspired, or improved your field.
3. **Consistency:** A clear timeline of success showing long-term achievement, not one lucky event.

If you can prove those three, your profession can qualify.

J. How to Build an Extraordinary Profile (Even Before You Apply)

If you're not there yet, start *today*:

- Publish your work (articles, videos, courses, or designs).
- Speak at conferences or community events.
- Apply for awards and nominations.
- Collaborate with recognized professionals.
- Document everything every photo, article, and invitation counts.

Your file should tell a story: that your journey is not ordinary. It's the story of someone whose work inspires change and whose name will carry weight even before USCIS reads it.

K. The Message for Dreamers and Achievers

The EB-1A category is not just an immigration path it's a mirror. It reflects the best version of who you are and what you have built. Every immigrant who creates, teaches, heals, or leads has the potential to rise into this category.

You don't have to marry anyone or depend on anyone. You just have to **believe that your talent is your visa** and build the evidence to prove it.

Marriage Is Not the **Option to Get a Green Card Anymore**

Chapter 11

The Right Careers That Commonly Qualify for EB-2 NIW Self-petition

The EB-2 NIW (Employment-Based Second Preference – National Interest Waiver) is a U.S. immigration category that allows certain highly qualified foreign nationals to apply for a green card on their own without a job offer or employer sponsorship when their professional work benefits the national interest of the United States.

"National Interest Waiver" means that the U.S. government waives the usual job-offer and labor-certification requirements because your knowledge, skills, or contributions are considered so valuable that the country wants you to continue your work freely.

To qualify, an applicant must show three things:

1. Their field of work has substantial merit and national importance (for example, improving health, technology, education, or the economy).

2. They are well positioned to advance that work through education, experience, or past achievements.
3. Granting the waiver would benefit the United States more than forcing the person to go through traditional employer sponsorship.

In simple terms, the EB-2 NIW is for people whose career creates a positive impact beyond their own success professionals, innovators, educators, entrepreneurs, or community leaders whose work moves the nation forward.

1. Healthcare & Public Health

The U.S. strongly prioritizes any work that improves public health, especially in underserved areas.

Typical Professions

- Medical doctors and surgeons
- Nurses, nurse practitioners, and physician assistants
- Dentists and public health educators
- Pharmacists and laboratory scientists
- Epidemiologists and health policy experts
- Nutritionists, dietitians, and mental-health therapists

Why They Qualify Their services directly affect the national health system, rural access to care, and emergency response capacity.

Evidence Examples

- Medical licenses and degrees

- Records of service in shortage areas (HPSA or MUA)
- Research or health program results
- Letters from hospitals, clinics, or public health agencies

2. Science, Engineering & Technology

STEM professionals are among the strongest NIW applicants because innovation and infrastructure are national priorities.

Typical Professions

- Civil, mechanical, electrical, and environmental engineers
- Software developers and data scientists
- Renewable-energy and sustainability specialists
- AI, robotics, and cybersecurity experts
- Researchers in biotechnology, chemistry, or materials science

Why They Qualify Their innovations help advance U.S. competitiveness, safety, and infrastructure resilience.

Evidence Examples

- Patents or published research
- Documentation of projects improving technology or safety
- Participation in U.S. or international collaborations
- Articles, conference invitations, or awards

3. Education & Academic Development

Education reform and workforce development are considered matters of national interest.

Typical Professions

- Teachers, professors, and curriculum developers
- Educational consultants and policy researchers
- Special-education experts or bilingual program creators
- Founders of community or adult-learning initiatives

Why They Qualify They address the nation's educational gaps, literacy, and immigrant integration through learning.

Evidence Examples

- Publications or educational materials used by schools
- Statistics showing program outcomes or student reach
- Letters from school boards, NGOs, or education departments

4. Business, Entrepreneurship & Economics

Entrepreneurs who create U.S. jobs or strengthen trade links can use EB-2 NIW to stay and grow their ventures.

Typical Professions

- Startup founders, business consultants, or import/export specialists

- Economists, market analysts, or logistics professionals
- Social entrepreneurs working with minority or immigrant communities

Why They Qualify Their activities generate employment, tax revenue, and local economic growth.

Evidence Examples

- Business registration, contracts, and financial reports
- Job creation statistics or letters from partners
- Media coverage or awards recognizing impact

5. Agriculture, Environment & Sustainability

The U.S. values experts improving food security and environmental protection.

Typical Professions

- Agronomists, soil scientists, and food technologists
- Environmental engineers or ecologists
- Renewable-energy researchers (solar, wind, water)
- Waste-management and recycling specialists

Why They Qualify They contribute to national sustainability, resource security, and climate goals.

Evidence Examples

- Project documentation or patents
- Collaboration with universities or government agencies
- Reports showing environmental or community results

6. Law, Policy & Human Rights

Legal or policy professionals whose work improves justice, governance, or immigrant integration can qualify if their impact extends beyond private clients.

Typical Professions

- Public-interest lawyers and immigration advocates
- Policy analysts and human-rights researchers
- Nonprofit directors or social-justice program coordinators

Why They Qualify They serve the national interest by improving systems of fairness, access, and civil protection.

Evidence Examples

- Published reports or legal research cited by institutions
- Awards or recognition for community impact
- Letters from government or NGO partners

7. Arts, Media & Cultural Development

Creative professionals may qualify if their work promotes U.S. culture, diversity, or international understanding.

Typical Professions

- Journalists, authors, and documentary filmmakers
- Cultural producers, museum curators, or event organizers
- Designers, chefs, or artists influencing cultural innovation

Why They Qualify They enhance America's global image, multicultural dialogue, and creative economy.

Evidence Examples

- Media coverage or exhibition records
- Cultural program outcomes or international recognition
- Testimonials from industry experts

8. Social Work, Psychology & Community Leadership

Service-oriented professionals are often approved when their work improves vulnerable populations' well-being.

Typical Professions

- Social workers, therapists, and youth counselors
- Community organizers or nonprofit founders

- Public-safety or rehabilitation specialists

Why They Qualify They promote social stability and public welfare core elements of national interest.

Evidence Examples

- Program impact data (numbers served, success rates)
- Letters from community leaders or government officials
- Grants or awards for community service

9. Infrastructure & Urban Development

Specialists improving transportation, housing, or urban systems help sustain U.S. growth.

Typical Professions

- Urban planners, architects, and construction managers
- Transportation or energy-grid engineers
- Housing or disaster-recovery experts

Why They Qualify They strengthen critical infrastructure and resilience to natural or economic challenges.

Evidence Examples

- Blueprints or reports of completed projects
- Collaboration with public agencies
- Recognition for sustainable or innovative design

10. Public Safety, Defense & Cybersecurity

Experts who enhance national security through technology or operations qualify under NIW due to direct government interest.

Typical Professions

- Cybersecurity analysts, data-protection specialists
- Emergency-management professionals
- Homeland-security or public-safety trainers

Why They Qualify They reduce risks, protect data, and improve readiness across the U.S.

Evidence Examples

- Certifications, training records, or incident-response results
- Letters from defense or government partners
- Publications or patents in security technologies

11. Faith-Based & Humanitarian Leadership

When spiritual or humanitarian work reaches communities in need, it can meet NIW standards.

Typical Professions

- Faith-based organization founders or directors
- Mission coordinators providing relief, education, or health services

- International aid consultants

Why They Qualify They deliver measurable social and moral benefit to vulnerable populations.

Evidence Examples

- Nonprofit registration and activity reports
- Letters from beneficiaries or partner organizations
- News coverage or awards recognizing humanitarian results

In Summary

EB-2 NIW is open to **any career that provides measurable public value**.

If your work:

1. Solves a problem of national importance,
2. Demonstrates clear results or leadership, and
3. Needs freedom from employer sponsorship to continue,

then you may qualify.

"The EB-2 NIW is not about titles it's about impact."

You don't need to be a celebrity or a CEO. You need to prove that your contribution in medicine, art, business, education, or community service **helps America move forward**.

Chapter 12

Important Legal Clarification for Overstays and Unlawful Entry

A. The Truth About Status vs. Petition

Many immigrants mistakenly believe that once USCIS approves their **employment-based petition** whether **EB-1, EB-2, EB-3, or EB-2 NIW** they have automatically gained legal status or a green card. That is **not true.**

Approval of a petition (Form I-140) simply means the government recognizes your *qualifications* and agrees you are eligible to apply for permanent residency **in principle**. However, **adjustment of status (Form I-485)** the step that grants the actual green card is a **separate legal process** with strict eligibility rules.

In other words:

> "Having your petition approved is recognition; getting your status adjusted is authorization."

B. If You Have Overstayed Your Visa

If you entered the United States **legally** for example, with a visitor, student, or work visa but **remained after your authorized stay expired**, here's what applies:

1. **You may still file Form I-140** (Immigrant Petition for Alien Worker). This allows USCIS to evaluate and approve your EB-1, EB-2, or NIW petition based on your education, skills, or contributions. Your overstay does not block your ability to file or receive an I-140 approval.

2. **However, you cannot file Form I-485** (Adjustment of Status) **from inside the U.S.** unless one of the following applies:

    - You **currently hold a lawful status** (for example, your visa is still valid or you have TPS or parole status).
    - You qualify under a **special exception**, such as:
        - **VAWA (Violence Against Women Act)** self-petitioners;
        - **Section 245(i)** grandfathering (if a qualifying petition was filed before April 30, 2001);

- **Temporary Protected Status (TPS)** holders who traveled abroad and re-entered with **advance parole.**

3. **Bars to Reentry After Overstay**

    - If you overstayed **more than 180 days**, leaving the U.S. triggers a **3-year bar** before you can reenter.
    - If you overstayed **more than one year**, it triggers a **10-year bar.** These bars apply even if your petition is approved.

Example: Maritza entered the U.S. with a visitor visa, applied for EB-2 NIW, and received I-140 approval. However, she overstayed for 14 months. If she leaves the country to process her visa abroad, she will face a **10-year re-entry bar** unless she obtains a waiver (Form I-601 or I-601A).

C. If You Entered Without Inspection (EWI)

If you entered the U.S. **without inspection** meaning you crossed the border or entered without a valid visa your situation is more complex, but not impossible.

1. **You can still file and get I-140 approval.** USCIS may approve your EB-1 or EB-2 NIW petition, recognizing your merit or contributions. However, this approval does **not grant you legal presence** or the right to stay.
2. **You cannot adjust your status inside the U.S.** unless you later become "admitted or paroled." This can happen through:

- **TPS travel authorization** (Advance Parole under Temporary Protected Status),
- **Parole in Place (for family of U.S. military members),** or
- **A waiver of inadmissibility** that allows you to process your case abroad.

Example: Carlos entered the U.S. without inspection in 2010 and later qualified for EB-2 NIW. His I-140 was approved, but he cannot apply for adjustment of status inside the U.S. until he travels under parole or completes consular processing with a waiver.

D. Waivers and Paths to Forgiveness

If your petition is approved but you cannot adjust status because of unlawful presence or entry, you may still have a path forward through **a waiver** a legal pardon that forgives your violation.

1. Form I-601 – Waiver of Grounds of Inadmissibility

Filed **from outside the U.S.**, usually after your consular interview. You must prove **extreme hardship** to a **U.S. citizen or lawful permanent resident spouse or parent.**

2. Form I-601A – Provisional Unlawful Presence Waiver

Filed **while inside the U.S.**, before departing for the interview abroad. It allows you to obtain advance forgiveness for unlawful presence to minimize separation time.

Once the waiver is approved, you can:

- Complete **consular processing** abroad, then return legally as a permanent resident; or
- In some cases, if you qualify under specific humanitarian or parole provisions, **adjust status inside the U.S.**

E. The Role of Parole and Reentry Authorization

If you hold **Temporary Protected Status (TPS)** or another humanitarian program, you may request **Advance Parole** (Form I-131). When you reenter the U.S. legally under that parole, you are considered **"inspected and admitted"**, which may make you **eligible to adjust status** after an EB-2 NIW or EB-1 approval.

This strategy has allowed many long-term TPS holders and DACA recipients to finally apply for their green card **without leaving the country**.

F. The Importance of Legal Strategy

Employment-based petitions are powerful tools but they must be combined with a **status strategy**. A strong EB-1 or EB-2 NIW approval proves your professional value; a waiver, parole, or adjustment process proves your **legal admissibility**.

The two are separate pillars that must work together.

G. A Message to Every Dreamer and Professional

If you overstayed, entered without inspection, or made a mistake do not lose hope. Immigration law recognizes that people evolve, contribute, and rebuild. Your past does not erase your merit, but you must walk the legal steps carefully.

> "A brilliant mind can win a petition, but only a wise plan can win a green card."

When you combine achievement with lawful process documentation, waiver, and strategy your story becomes more than survival. It becomes a testimony of transformation, discipline, and grace.

Chapter 13

The Waiver of Inadmissibility: A Second Chance Through Form I-601 or I-601A

A. What the Waiver Means

The **Waiver of Inadmissibility** is one of the most compassionate remedies in U.S. immigration law. It is designed to help people who made mistakes, overstayed, or violated certain rules but who still have strong family or humanitarian reasons to stay connected to the United States.

Through **Form I-601** or **Form I-601A**, you can ask the U.S. government to **forgive specific immigration violations**, such as:

- **Unlawful presence** (staying in the U.S. beyond the period of authorized stay),
- **Certain misrepresentations or fraud** at entry,

- **Some criminal grounds** (in limited, non-serious cases), or
- **Health-related or documentation-related issues** preventing admissibility.

A waiver doesn't erase the past, but it allows you to **move forward legally and rebuild your life.**

B. The Legal Basis "Extreme Hardship"

To qualify, you must demonstrate that denying your admission would cause **extreme hardship** to a **qualifying relative** usually your **U.S. citizen or lawful permanent resident spouse or parent**. (Children do *not* qualify on their own for this hardship requirement.)

Extreme hardship means more than emotional pain.

It can include:

- Financial loss or inability to meet obligations;
- Medical conditions requiring your support or care;
- Educational disruption for dependent family members;
- Psychological suffering or trauma;
- Country conditions that would endanger your family abroad.

You must prove that your qualifying relative would face exceptional, unusual, or severe consequences if you were forced to leave or remain separated.

C. The Two Types of Waivers

1. Form I-601 – Waiver of Grounds of Inadmissibility

This is filed by people **outside the U.S.** or those already in consular processing after a denial or inadmissibility finding.

You typically:

1. Attend a consular interview abroad,
2. Receive notice of inadmissibility,
3. File **Form I-601** with evidence of extreme hardship,
4. Wait for USCIS approval before returning to complete visa issuance.

Example: Jean entered the U.S. unlawfully and later married a U.S. citizen. Because he must complete his immigrant visa interview abroad, he files **Form I-601** to request forgiveness for his unlawful presence, showing that his U.S. citizen wife depends on him emotionally and financially.

2. Form I-601A – Provisional Unlawful Presence Waiver

This special version is for people **still inside the United States** who only need forgiveness for **unlawful presence** (not other violations). It allows them to **apply for the waiver before leaving** for their immigrant visa interview abroad.

This helps families avoid long separations, since once approved, the applicant can travel for the consular interview knowing the waiver has already been granted.

Example: Maria overstayed her visa for several years but married a U.S. citizen. She filed **Form I-601A** while still in the U.S., proving that her husband would suffer extreme hardship without her. Once approved, she traveled to her home country, completed the visa interview, and returned as a permanent resident all within months, not years.

D. Evidence That Strengthens a Waiver Case

To succeed, you must **document the hardship** with precision and compassion.

Typical evidence includes:

- Medical reports and doctor letters for the qualifying relative;
- Psychological evaluations detailing emotional impact;
- Financial records showing dependence or loss;
- Country condition reports (violence, instability, lack of medical care);
- Photos, affidavits, and personal letters describing family unity.

A well-prepared waiver tells a **human story supported by legal facts** not just emotions but *evidence of why separation would destroy stability.*

E. The Process

1. **Determine Eligibility** – Identify which waiver applies (I-601 or I-601A).
2. **Gather Evidence** – Document every hardship element.
3. **File with USCIS** – Submit the correct form, fee, and evidence packet.
4. **Wait for Decision** – Processing can take 6–18 months, depending on the case.
5. **Consular Interview or Adjustment of Status** – If approved, complete the process to receive your immigrant visa or green card.

F. The Meaning Behind the Waiver

Beyond legal procedure, a waiver represents **mercy, fairness, and second chances.** It recognizes that good people can make mistakes that families deserve unity, and that love, care, and contribution to society should not be erased by a past misstep.

> "A waiver is not a loophole. It's a bridge between what went wrong and what can be made right."

For many immigrants, this form restores hope it allows them to step out of fear and into legal stability, guided by compassion and proof that their family and their presence matter to the nation they now call home.

▯ In Short

Situation	Can You Adjust Inside the U.S.?	Notes
Entered legally, overstayed	☑ Possibly, with lawful status or exceptions	If inspected & admitted, you may adjust when visa is available
Entered without inspection (EWI)	✖ Usually no	Must leave for consular interview even after waiver
Entered without inspection but later re-entered with parole (TPS/DACA)	☑ Yes	Now considered "inspected," eligible for adjustment
Protected by 245(i)	☑ Yes	Can adjust with penalty fee
Filed VAWA, U Visa, or Asylum	☑ Often yes	Depends on specific case

Chapter 14

How to Become an Asset in the System to Qualify for the EB Category Self-Petition Green Card

A. What It Truly Means to Be an Asset

Being an *asset* means your presence strengthens the nation. You bring value not just through your skills, but through your discipline, integrity, leadership, and financial responsibility.

To USCIS and society, the most valuable immigrant is not only one with talent, but one who demonstrates trustworthiness, stability, and contribution.

You become an asset when your name represents reliability. When people officials, employers, or your own community can say:

> "This person adds value wherever they go."

B. The Three Pillars of Value: Skill, Integrity, and Stability

To qualify for EB-1 or EB-2 NIW, you must demonstrate three kinds of strength:

1. Professional Strength: Education, experience, achievements, and impact in your field.
2. Moral Strength: Good character, respect for the law, honesty, and responsibility.
3. Financial Strength: Stability, good money management, and reliability in obligations.

When these three align, you are not just qualified you are *trusted.*

C. Character: The Foundation of All Success

USCIS often refers to "good moral character," and it is one of the most powerful assets you can have. Good character builds credibility in ways no document can replace.

To live as a person of integrity:

- Avoid all legal trouble no arrests, no altercations, no lies on immigration forms.
- Keep your records honest pay your taxes faithfully and report income truthfully.
- Stay away from drugs, illegal activity, or anything that puts your name in danger.

- Speak and act with respect. Even small moments of kindness build a powerful reputation.

Good moral character is not about perfection it's about consistency. It is the quiet, daily decision to do what's right even when no one is watching.

D. Presentation: Your Professional Image Speaks First

Presentation is not vanity; it is respect for yourself, for others, and for the opportunities you are asking for.

1. Dress with Purpose. Clean, professional, and simple always wins.
2. Be Organized. Keep your documents, home, and finances in order.
3. Communicate Clearly. Speak with grace and confidence, not arrogance or fear.
4. Be Punctual. Arriving on time shows responsibility lateness shows carelessness.
5. Stay Humble. Confidence attracts opportunity; arrogance repels it.

You don't need to look rich to look respectable. You need to look responsible.

E. Financial Responsibility: Becoming a True Economic Asset

The way you manage money says a lot about your ability to manage your life. Financial responsibility is part of moral character. It shows maturity, foresight, and discipline.

1. Pay Your Debts and Bills on Time. Even small unpaid balances can affect your credit score and reputation. USCIS and consulates respect people who fulfill their financial obligations.

2. Avoid Unnecessary Debt. Use credit wisely. Build credit, don't bury yourself in it. Show that you know how to manage resources not just request them.

3. File and Pay Taxes Honestly. Paying taxes demonstrates responsibility and good faith to the U.S. system. Keep all receipts, W-2s, or 1099s as evidence of contribution.

4. Build Stability, Not Just Income. Save regularly, live within your means, and plan for emergencies. Stability impresses officers as much as success.

5. Invest in Growth, Not Image. Education, training, and lawful business ventures are real assets. Expensive clothes or cars are temporary impressions knowledge is lasting wealth.

Being financially responsible is part of your *evidence of integration.* It tells the system: "I am not a risk. I am a resource."

F. Your Social and Public Image: Reputation Is Power

In the digital age, social media is part of your reputation. An immigration officer may not officially "follow" you, but your online behavior builds your professional image in the eyes of the world.

Golden Rules for a Respectful Online Presence:

1. Be Respectful. Don't post offensive, angry, or vulgar content.
2. Be Purposeful. Share your professional work, achievements, or community involvement.
3. Be Peaceful. Avoid political arguments, gossip, or drama.
4. Be Authentic. Use your platform to inspire and uplift, not to show off or compete.
5. Be Mindful. Remember, what you post can live forever let it reflect pride and positivity.

Your reputation is your silent reference letter. Every post, every comment, every photo should answer this question:

"Would I be proud if this appeared next to my name on my petition?"

G. Leadership and Community Involvement

An *asset* is not someone who stands alone it's someone who elevates others.

You become more valuable to society when you:

- Volunteer in community organizations or church programs.
- Mentor others in your profession or immigrant circle.
- Teach, guide, or advocate for fair treatment and education.
- Represent your homeland with excellence and humility.

Leadership is not about titles; it's about impact. The more people you help, the stronger your case for being "in the national interest."

H. Combining Excellence, Character, and Stability

To truly stand out as an immigrant asset:

Area	Action	Result
Character	Live by integrity, honesty, and respect	Builds trust and moral credibility
Presentation	Keep a clean, professional image	Projects confidence and reliability
Social Image	Use social media with purpose	Strengthens your public reputation
Financial Stability	Manage money, pay taxes, avoid debt	Demonstrates responsibility and foresight
Leadership	Serve and uplift others	Shows that you add measurable value to the U.S.

This combination makes you not just a qualified immigrant but a model citizen in training.

I. The Personal Code of Conduct for the Modern Immigrant

(A Daily Standard for Leadership, Integrity, and Excellence)

1. I live in integrity and obey the law.
2. I maintain a clean, disciplined, and respectful appearance.
3. I honor my financial responsibilities and avoid unnecessary debt.
4. I speak truth and respect in all my communication.
5. I use social media wisely, building others, not dividing them.
6. I work with excellence and gratitude in all I do.
7. I invest in learning, growth, and service to my community.
8. I keep my record, finances, and personal life organized.
9. I represent my homeland with pride, grace, and humility.
10. I walk each day in faith, confidence, and divine purpose.

"The world may not know your story yet, but your character will introduce you before your résumé does." Ruth Michel-Dupoux

---

J. Final Reflection: The Real Definition of Success

Becoming an asset to this country is not only about proving your worth on paper it's about becoming the kind of person whose presence makes life better for others.

When you walk in discipline, live in integrity, and handle your responsibilities with excellence, you become more than a qualified immigrant you become a pillar of trust, leadership, and inspiration.

Success is not when your papers are approved; success is when your life reflects the reason they should be.

Live as proof that immigrants build nations. Be the example of strength, respect, and faith that others can follow. Because when you become an asset in every way morally, socially, and financially no door can stay closed for long.

This book does not create an attorney-client relationship. Immigration laws change, and outcomes vary by case. Readers should consult USCIS, DHS, DOJ, or qualified legal professionals before making decisions.

My Personal Commitment to Become an Asset

(A Promise of Integrity, Discipline, and Purpose)

Today, I made a conscious decision to rise above fear, confusion, and dependency. I understand that my journey in this country is not just about survival, it's about **becoming an example** of excellence, leadership, and faith.

From this day forward, I choose to live as an **asset**, someone whose presence adds value, whose actions inspire respect, and whose character earns trust.

I will honor the laws of this country and respect those who serve it. I will maintain a clean record, a disciplined lifestyle, and a professional appearance that reflects self-respect and purpose. I will use my talents and skills to build, not to complain; to uplift, not to divide.

I will manage my finances with wisdom, paying my bills, reducing debt, and planning for stability, because financial order is part of moral order. I will use social media and my voice responsibly, understanding that my influence is a reflection of my values.

I will walk in humility, speak with kindness, and work with excellence. I will mentor, serve, and lead wherever I am planted, knowing that greatness begins with good character.

I understand that my actions today will speak louder than any words tomorrow. Therefore, I choose to walk in truth, to lead with love, and to trust God's divine plan for my life.

> *"I am not just seeking opportunity, I am becoming one."*

Signature: ____________________ **Date:** ________________________

Name: ____

Personal Reflection:

What steps will I take this month to strengthen my life as an asset? (Write your goals below.)

11. ____

12. ____

13. ____

14. ____

Faith, Truth, and Patience

A Personal Reflection and Disclaimer

Every immigration story is different. Every path, no matter how similar it may seem, is deeply personal and shaped by unique facts, history, and timing.

Some will receive answers quickly; others will face long periods of waiting, silence, or unexpected turns. Yet no journey is wasted when it is walked in faith, truth, and patience.

Even when mistakes have been made an overstay, a missed deadline, a wrong form there is still room for forgiveness in the system. Waivers, humanitarian protections, and appeals exist for a reason: to restore fairness and hope where fear once lived.

But it is important to remember that **this book does not replace professional legal advice.** Immigration law is complex and constantly changing. The information and examples shared here are meant to **educate and empower**, not to serve as specific legal instruction for any individual case.

If you are facing deportation, unlawful presence, or an uncertain status, always consult a **licensed immigration attorney or accredited legal**

representative who can analyze your full situation and guide you through the proper legal process.

Faith is not only for prayer it is also for perseverance. Keep your papers truthful, your words consistent, and your intentions pure. Do not be afraid to seek help, to ask questions, or to begin again.

Because no matter how complicated the road may look, the truth always opens doors that lies and shortcuts will close. And when you walk your journey with patience and integrity, you'll discover that the door which once seemed shut can, in time, open again not by luck, but by **purpose, courage, and divine grace.**

Conclusion: Choose Freedom, Not Fear

Marriage is sacred but it should never be a transaction. Throughout this journey, we've seen how many immigrants have suffered emotionally, psychologically, and spiritually by tying their dreams to someone else's decisions. We've also seen that there are other ways, lawful, dignified, and empowering ways to build your future.

Marriage is not your only option. Love should never be a condition for legality, nor should dependency replace dignity. The U.S. immigration system may be complex, but it offers paths that reward integrity, talent, and faith.

Your story does not end in waiting, tears, or abuse. It begins when you decide to rise to build, to learn, to lead, and to walk by faith. Your green card should never come from fear; it should come from purpose.

You came here not to survive, but to contribute. Not to be tolerated, but to be trusted. Not to depend, but to develop.

Believe that God's plan for you includes peace, prosperity, and purpose not pain. You are not a burden; you are a blessing. And your journey, with honesty and perseverance, will become your greatest testimony.

The truth is, God didn't bring you to this country to be someone's prisoner. He brought you here to fulfill your purpose. Whether through education, entrepreneurship, service, or leadership, you have the power to contribute, to build, and to belong.

Let this be your turning point. No more waiting for someone else to "save" you. No more sacrificing your dignity for documents. You can choose integrity. You can choose independence. You can choose *freedom over fear.*

The United States was built by people who believed in dreams and you, too, are part of that story. Stand tall. Do things the right way. Become a builder, not a burden. Be a light in your community. Live with faith, honesty, and gratitude because the same God who brought you this far will never leave you now.

Introduction to the Immigrant's Prayers

Every immigrant carries two suitcases one filled with documents, and one filled with dreams. Between those two, there is always a space where only faith can live.

These prayers were born from that space the quiet moments between fear and hope, between rejection letters and new beginnings. They are not written as religious rituals, but as conversations with God, whispered from the heart of every man and woman who has ever left everything behind to start over.

Immigration is more than a legal process; it is an act of courage, sacrifice, and faith. We pray when the papers are delayed, when the answers are uncertain, when the nights feel long and the waiting feels endless. We pray for our families back home, for our children's future, and for the strength to keep believing when the system feels too heavy to bear.

This collection of Immigrant's Prayers is a reminder that faith is not just a belief it's a strategy. It is what keeps our hearts steady when the laws change, when the interviews intimidate, and when the world doubts our worth.

Each prayer in this section was written for a different moment in the immigrant journey for courage, for forgiveness, for protection, for gratitude, and for victory. Some are inspired by my own experiences as a woman who had to rebuild her life in a foreign land, with only my faith, my work, and my purpose as my foundation.

May these words comfort you when you feel alone, lift you when you feel forgotten, and remind you that you are never invisible in God's plan. Your journey has meaning. Your story has power. And your faith even in silence is being heard.

So before you read the first prayer, take a deep breath. Close your eyes. Remember why you came, and who you are becoming.

> "Faith is the passport that cannot expire, and prayer is the visa that never runs out."

The Immigrant's Morning Prayer (For Strength and Divine Protection)

Heavenly Father,

As the sun rises, I lift my heart to You in gratitude. Thank You for the gift of a new day, for the breath in my lungs, and for the unseen mercies that carried me through the night. You brought me to this land not by chance, but by divine assignment. Even when I feel like a stranger, I know I am still a child of purpose, chosen, covered, and protected by Your hand.

Walk before me today, Lord. Go where I cannot go, and fight the battles I cannot see. Shield me from every threat from danger, deception, discrimination, and despair. Let no weapon formed against me prosper. Surround me with Your presence so powerfully that fear has no room to live within me.

Let Your angels stand guard over my path in the streets, in my workplace, in every place my feet may go. Guard my home, my papers, my peace, and my name. Hide me under the shadow of Your wings where no harm can reach me.

Let my hands produce honest work that honors You. Let my words carry truth, my actions show grace, and my presence brings light wherever I go. Grant me wisdom to recognize what is from You and courage to walk away from what is not.

When confusion rises, let Your Spirit whisper direction. When I am tired, refill me with strength that only You can give.

Bless my family near and far and let Your protection cover them as well. Provide for their needs, comfort their hearts, and keep them safe from every danger.

Open the doors that are meant for me, Lord, and close the ones that would lead me astray. Let Your favor go before me in every appointment, interview, or application. Turn obstacles into opportunities and silence every voice that speaks against my destiny.

Let today be a day of peace, productivity, and divine protection. Let me walk with confidence, not because life is easy, but because I know who walks beside me.

In your holy name, I claim victory, safety, and favor over this day.

Amen.

The Immigrant's Night Prayer

Gracious Lord,

As I lay my head to rest, I thank You for carrying me through another day. Even when the road feels long, uncertain, and heavy, Your hand sustains me.

Forgive me for my doubts, my fears, and the moments when I lose strength. Renew my faith, refill my heart with courage, and remind me that every waiting season serves a purpose.

Protect my loved ones, near and far and bring peace to every immigrant searching for stability, safety, and a place to belong. Calm every anxious thought that tries to steal my rest. Let Your angels surround my home and cover me with divine protection.

I trust that You see what I cannot, that You are working even in silence, and that my journey is not in vain. You are my provider when doors close, my protector when the way feels dangerous, and my peace when uncertainty rises.

Forgive me for my panic, my sleepless nights, and the tears I hide behind my strength. Remind me that **You are greater than any badge, any system, any wall.** Your protection reaches where human mercy cannot.

Lord, give me courage for tomorrow, the courage to keep working, to keep believing, to keep walking in dignity no matter who watches.. Let every sound outside remind me not of danger, but of Your promise to never leave nor forsake me.

Watch over me tonight, Lord, and prepare my heart for tomorrow. Let Your favor go before me in every appointment, interview, or application. And when my victory comes, may my story bring glory to Your name not because of my strength, but because of Your grace.

Amen.

The Immigrant's Prayer for Strength While Waiting

(While My Papers Are Being Processed)

Heavenly Father,

You know the weight my heart carries today. My papers are in the hands of people I may never meet, yet I know that you can reach hearts, shift minds, and open doors even in government offices. You see every document I have sent every form signed, every translation prepared, every proof gathered with trembling hope.

Lord, I have done my part. Now I place the rest in Your hands. Touch the heart of the person reviewing my file. Let them see not just papers, but a life, a human story of sacrifice, honesty, and perseverance. Move through every desk, every folder, every system, and let my name find favor in the right hands.

Give me strength in this waiting season, because waiting is not easy. Some nights I worry that something will go wrong. Some mornings I refresh my case number, hoping to see a new update. But I know you are working, even when the screen is silent. You are the God of timing and truth. You never lose a file.

Teach me to wait with peace instead of panic. Remind me that what belongs to me will not be lost, and what is delayed is not denied. Let every obstacle in this process become an opportunity for testimony. If there is any missing piece, bring it to light. If there is confusion, bring clarity. If there is a human error, let it be corrected with mercy.

Bless the officer, the clerk, the adjudicator, and every person who touches my case. Let compassion fill their heart, fairness guide their decision, and grace go before every word they write. And if my file lands on a desk today, let Your Spirit whisper truth and kindness over my name.

While I wait, Lord, give me peace that passes understanding. Keep me productive, grateful, and faithful using this time to grow, not to fear. Help me believe that this process is part of my preparation, not my punishment.

And when the day comes when the decision arrives and the letter is opened let it bring tears of joy, not sorrow. Let it remind me that no system is too strong, no delay too long, for You to move on behalf of Your children.

Let Your favor go before me in every appointment, interview, or application. Turn this waiting season into a testimony of Your perfect will.

In your mighty name, I release my anxiety, trust Your timing, and thank You for the victory that is already written in Heaven.

Amen.

The Immigrant's Prayer for Victory and New Beginnings

Faithful Father,

Today my heart overflows with gratitude. The waiting is over, the door has opened, and the papers I prayed over are now marked *approved*. What felt impossible is now a testimony of Your mercy and power. You turned anxiety into peace, delays into destiny, and sleepless nights into songs of praise.

Thank You for every tear that watered this victory. Thank You for every prayer that reminded me not to give up. I may have walked through seasons of fear, but Your hand guided me through them all. You proved once again that your timing is perfect, never late, never early, always right on time.

Lord, I lift up every officer, every person who processed my case, every stranger who chose fairness and compassion. Bless them for being instruments of justice and grace. And bless me now as I begin this new chapter, one not built on fear, but on purpose.

As I step into this new beginning, let me not forget the lessons learned in the valley. Let me remain humble, kind, and grateful. Help me use this freedom not only to rebuild my life, but to uplift others who are still waiting, still hoping, still believing. Let my story give strength to those who feel forgotten.

Cover my new steps, Lord my work, my home, my travels, my future. Let every plan I make align with Your will. Protect me from pride, from complacency, and from any threat that would try to steal my peace. Let Your favor go before me in every new opportunity, meeting, and decision. Remind me daily that I did not come this far by chance, I came this far by grace.

And when I look back one day, let me see that every delay, every challenge, every sleepless night was part of the preparation for this moment.

This is not just my victory, it is Yours. So I dedicate this new season to You, Lord. May my life, my success, and my story always glorify Your name.

Amen.

From the Author's Heart

My dear reader,

If you have reached this page, it means you are looking for something deeper, maybe peace, maybe direction, or maybe just a reason to keep believing. I want you to know that your past does not define you. Your mistakes do not cancel your mission. And your pain, no matter how heavy, is not the end of your story.

I know this because I have walked that same road. I left behind everything familiar, my family, my language, my identity, to start over in a country that promised opportunity but often delivered silence and fear. I have sat in offices where people judged me by my accent, doubted my ability, and told me what I could *not* become. I have felt the weight of immigration papers that seemed to decide my destiny, and the loneliness of rebuilding from nothing while pretending to be strong.

But every time I thought I had reached the end, Grace whispered, *"Get up again."* Every time someone closed a door, faith reminded me that another one was waiting.

I built my life, piece by piece, as a woman, as an immigrant, as a paralegal, and as a voice for others who couldn't yet speak for themselves. I learned that our value does not come from where we were born, but from what we are willing to become. And I discovered that truth, when spoken with courage, can open doors that fear keeps locked.

You, too, were chosen for more. You came to this land not by chance, but by divine design. The same God who gave you the courage to cross oceans and borders will give you the wisdom to rise and rebuild.

Every delay, every rejection, every disappointment is not punishment, it's preparation. You are being shaped for a greater purpose. So lift your head, fix your papers, speak life over yourself, and keep walking in integrity.

Do your work with excellence. Tell your story without shame. And when your time comes, because it will and don't forget to turn back and lift someone else. Real success is not measured by what we achieve; it's measured by the lives we touch.

My prayer is that this book becomes more than information; it becomes your confirmation that *you can start again, and this time, you can win.*

With love, faith, and deep gratitude, **Ruth Michel-Dupoux**
Entrepreneur, *Paralegal, Author, and Immigrant Advocate*

The End

(But Also, the Beginning)

This book is not just the end of a journey, it is the beginning of a new one. You have learned the truth, faced the system, and discovered that your freedom does not come from another person's signature, it comes from your own strength, faith, and preparation.

Every page was written with purpose, to educate, to awaken, and to remind you that your story has power. You are more than a visa number, more than a status, more than a struggle. You are the dream your ancestors prayed for. You are the living proof that courage can cross oceans and still stand tall.

If you take anything from these chapters, let it be this: You do not need to trade your dignity for stability. You do not need to depend on others for validation. You can rise, self-petition, and succeed, lawfully, boldly, and beautifully.

Your value is not determined by your papers but by your principles. Your worth is not in what you receive but in what you give. And your destiny is not in the hands of any government, it's in the hands of God.

As you close this book, may you open a new chapter of your life with vision, peace, and courage. May you use what you've learned to help others, to uplift your community, and to live as the best version of yourself.

Go forward with clarity, discipline, and divine confidence. And never forget, *you are not just in this country to survive; you are here to serve, to shine, and to succeed.*

With love and faith, Ruth Michel-Dupoux Entrepreneur, *Paralegal, Author, and Immigrant Advocate*

Disclaimer and Source Information

All immigration and legal information presented in this book is based on **publicly available, verified, and official U.S. government sources**. These materials were carefully reviewed and compiled to ensure accuracy and integrity at the time of publication.

The primary government entities that regulate, enforce, and interpret U.S. immigration laws include:

- **U.S. Citizenship and Immigration Services (USCIS)**: https://www.uscis.gov *Responsible for processing immigration benefits such as green cards, work permits, naturalization, asylum, and humanitarian programs.*
- **U.S. Department of Homeland Security (DHS)**: https://www.dhs.gov *Oversees national security and immigration enforcement through its main agencies: USCIS, ICE, and CBP.*
- **U.S. Immigration and Customs Enforcement (ICE)**: https://www.ice.gov *Handles immigration investigations, detention, deportation proceedings, and enforcement of immigration laws within the United States.*

- **U.S. Customs and Border Protection (CBP)**: https://www.cbp.gov *Manages the inspection and admission of travelers and goods at U.S. borders, ports, and airports.*
- **U.S. Department of State (DOS)**: https://travel.state.gov *Oversees U.S. embassies and consulates abroad, responsible for issuing visas, managing the Visa Bulletin, and guiding consular processing.*
- **U.S. Department of Justice (DOJ)**: https://www.justice.gov *Includes the Executive Office for Immigration Review (EOIR), which manages immigration courts and the Board of Immigration Appeals (BIA).*
- **Executive Office for Immigration Review (EOIR)**: https://www.justice.gov/eoir *Conducts immigration court hearings, reviews appeals, and interprets immigration law through administrative judges and the BIA.*
- **U.S. Department of Labor (DOL)**: https://www.dol.gov *Regulates labor certifications (PERM process), prevailing wage determinations, and employment-related visa requirements for immigrant and non-immigrant workers.*
- **U.S. Department of Health and Human Services (HHS)**: https://www.hhs.gov *Provides guidance on health-related inadmissibility grounds, vaccinations, and refugee or public health programs.*
- **Federal Register and the Code of Federal Regulations (CFR, Title 8)**: https://www.ecfr.gov *Contain the official rules, policies, and regulatory frameworks governing immigration benefits, enforcement, and adjudications.*
- **U.S. Immigration Courts and the Board of Immigration Appeals (BIA)** *Operate under the Department of Justice, providing*

review and due process for individuals facing removal or appealing immigration decisions.

Purpose of This Publication

This book was written for **educational, informational, and inspirational purposes only.** Its mission is to **help immigrants, students, and professionals understand lawful immigration options, build confidence, and navigate their journey with truth and faith.**

The author is not acting as an attorney or providing legal representation. All explanations, summaries, and examples are based on **general knowledge of U.S. immigration law** and are intended to **guide and empower readers**, not to serve as specific legal advice for individual cases.

Immigration law is complex and constantly evolving through federal legislation, administrative updates, and court decisions. Therefore, readers should always **verify current information** directly from the official U.S. government websites listed above or consult with a **licensed immigration attorney** or **DOJ-accredited representative** before taking legal action.

Good Faith and Integrity Statement

All materials in this book were compiled in **good faith** from credible, public, and government-verified sources. No confidential or proprietary information has been used. While every effort was made to ensure accuracy, the author and publisher **assume no responsibility for errors, changes in law, or misinterpretations of official guidance.**

This book is an act of service, not substitution. Its purpose is to inform, encourage, and awaken the immigrant spirit that chooses faith over fear and truth over confusion.

www.ingramcontent.com/pod-product-compliance
Lightning Source LLC
LaVergne TN
LVHW022223200926
848481LV00006B/2095
* 9 7 9 8 3 4 8 2 7 3 3 0 9 *